A Midsummer Night's Hangover

EUDAIMON PRESS
2010

A Midsummer Night's Hangover

Emile Benoit

To my three best girls, with much love
L.M.B.

Table of Contents

A Midsummer Night's Hangover

CHARACTERS

MAVERICK
Mid to late 20's; recent college graduate with an artistic and melancholy sensibility

GEMINI
20 years old; romantic idealist who is in love with Felicity

FELICITY
20 years old; Matthew's daughter; Pretty and bursting with life.

MATTHEW
50 years old; Felicity's father; stern and exacting; strongly religious.

GLORIA
Early 20's; rabidly feminist before there was such a thing; Felicity's best friend

JUDE
Early 20's; enamored with Gloria; naïve and gawky.

STATUE
30-50; Beautiful and elegant; playful; a bit of a lush.

A Midsummer Night's Hangover

SCENE 1

The street of a small farming community somewhere in rural
Europe circa 1962

(Enter Maverick and Gemini)

MAVERICK:

> What system of thought causes a mother
> to sing to her child? If she were to think
> on it might she not fall into despair?
> After all, the child begins to age
> as soon as it is born. She, too, is dying.
> And if she lives long enough to see him
> grown, invariably he must leave her.
> And this she knows, though she may deny it.
> Whyfor then the song? And why a tune so
> optimistic? A sound so full of hope?
> Her hymn is one of justice, though none she
> will receive. Of unity, though the two
> shall be forever split. Of eternal
> love, though by consequence she must relinquish
> it. Wherefrom springs her courage in the face
> of such a bitter foe? She fights against
> the forces of gravity and so, by
> leaping from these heights, her descent will show
> to be all the more crushing. Whyfor attempt
> it? These are deeds which confound our reason.
> Yet we understand them. For the soul doth know
> things for which even gods throw up their hands.

GEMINI:

> You know, that's very annoying.

MAVERICK:
> What?

GEMINI:
> Poetry. It's annoying.

MAVERICK:
> I'm sorry?

GEMINI:
> People don't normally break into verse. Except in
> Shakespeare. And even then it's annoying. Poetry is dead.

MAVERICK:
> No, chivalry is dead.

GEMINI:
> You should join us among the living sometime.

MAVERICK:
> I don't like the view. Besides, what's the use of living if
> poetry is dead?

GEMINI:
> You're such an elitist. I think I'm going to start calling you
> Moses from now on.

MAVERICK:
> Moses led his people out of slavery. My people enjoy
> being slaves.

GEMINI:
> How is it that I never seem to know what you're talking
> about?

MAVERICK:
You don't really want to know.

GEMINI:
You're probably right.

MAVERICK:
The truth is always an incredible disappointment.

GEMINI:
I'm glad to see that things haven't changed since you've been gone.

MAVERICK:
If I could just be depressed I'd be much happier, I think. I mean, there is a certain comfort in resignation. Instead, I sit at home and contemplate statues. There's this sculpture of a woman that I bought the other day. I haven't been able to get her off my mind.

GEMINI:
You think too much.

MAVERICK: *(melancholy)*
She's lasted through centuries. And someone hand-carved her. Out of rough stone. They took the elements of nature, mixed it with their soul and created this amazing work of art. A creative act which defies destruction. Where 'death shall have no dominion.' And I, for the life of me, cannot even conceive an original thought.

GEMINI:
That's quite a philosophy you're developing there. Did you pick that up at college?

MAVERICK:

> I'm still working on it. But I'm a realist. 'All life is but a fantasy ordained to make its sleeping dreamer smile'.

GEMINI:

> That's nice.

MAVERICK:

> I read it on a travel brochure somewhere.

GEMINI:

> Well, here we are.

MAVERICK:

> Can you tell me *now* what we're doing here?

GEMINI:

> Do you remember Felicity?

MAVERICK:

> Old man Matthew's daughter?

GEMINI:

> Every morning she and her father walk along this road. And we're going to meet up with them. Here.

MAVERICK:

> And why would we wish to do that?

GEMINI:

> I'm in love with her.

MAVERICK:

> Again?

GEMINI:
>I'm still in love with her. I've decided.

MAVERICK:
>You don't just decide you're in love.

GEMINI:
>I can't stop thinking about her.

MAVERICK:
>You hardly know the girl.

GEMINI:
>My father worked for old man Matthew in case you've forgotten.

MAVERICK:
>And in that time how often did you even speak to her? Once? Twice? Three times perhaps?

GEMINI:
>We spoke with our eyes.

MAVERICK:
>Oh, well, now see, you didn't tell me that.

GEMINI:
>I really think she loves me too.

MAVERICK:
>Are you aware that women are to some extent involved in nearly ninety-eight percent of all male suicides? The other two percent are monks without mothers.

GEMINI:
>Don't you think she's beautiful?

MAVERICK:
> That's not the point. I think you've forgotten about her father.

GEMINI:
> I've found a way around him.

MAVERICK: *(Teasing)*
> You've killed him?

GEMINI:
> I only want to be able to tell her how I feel, that's all.

> *(Enter Matthew and Felicity)*

MAVERICK:
> Here's your opportunity.

MATTHEW:
> Well, look who's here.

GEMINI:
> How are you, sir? Felicity.

MATTHEW:
> What is it that you want?

GEMINI:
> I'm just being neighborly.

MATTHEW: *(begins to leave)*
> Very well. God bless.

GEMINI:
> Sir? I wanted to thank you again for everything that you did for my father.

MATTHEW:
> How many times do you have to thank me for that? I'm sure that he'll thank me himself when my time comes, in heaven.

MAVERICK: *(dryly)*
> And when might he be expecting you?

MATTHEW:
> Laugh now, pigeon.

GEMINI:
> Sir, I'm trying to finally close the loose ends regarding my father's estate and there are a few things I need to discuss with you.

MATTHEW:
> It will have to wait. Felicity and I are already late for breakfast.

GEMINI:
> It's about your debt, sir.

MATTHEW:
> My debt? What are you talking about? What debt? Nevermind. We'll discuss it later. Come by the house.

GEMINI:
> Fine. How does this afternoon suit you?

MATTHEW:
> That'll be fine. Good day.

GEMINI:
> Good-bye, Felicity.

(Exit Matthew and Felicity)

MAVERICK:
How did you just manage an invitation to his house?

GEMINI:
All part of the plan, my friend.

MAVERICK:
You've a plan?

GEMINI:
My father gave Felicity a horse when she was young. He said it was because it reminded him of her. Who was the goddess that rode Pegasus? Athena? He said she reminded him of Athena. So he bought the horse, tied a bow around its neck, and presented it to Felicity as a present from her father. He knew Matthew would have never allowed it otherwise. In fact, Matthew was so upset that he insisted my father draw up a purchase agreement with interest in order to buy the horse himself. Not too long afterward, Matthew worked the horse to death on his farm. After that, I suppose everyone forgot about it.

MAVERICK:
Poor Felicity.

GEMINI:
However, I came upon the document while I was going over some of my father's things.

MAVERICK:
And you expect he's going to trade his daughter for it?

GEMINI:

>It got me in the door didn't it? At least I'll be able to talk to her finally.

MAVERICK:

>If we put as much effort into curing cancer as we do chasing after love...

GEMINI:

>When did you become so cynical?

MAVERICK:

>It's more of a calling than a choice.

(They exit)

SCENE 2
Felicity's Garden.

(Felicity and Gloria enter)

FELICITY:
> Oh, Gloria, you should have seen him. So handsome. The way he looked at me...I'm not entirely certain I still have my virginity.

GLORIA:
> Felicity!

FELICITY:
> It's been ten years, Gloria. Ten years. And do I even speak to him? No, suddenly I become as silent as a nun. Oh, why didn't I speak to him?

GLORIA:
> Your father would have killed you.

FELICITY:
> It feels like I'm dying now.

GLORIA:
> Oh, poppycock. Your hormones are playing tricks on you.

FELICITY:
> He touched my hand, did I tell you?

GLORIA:
> When? This morning?

FELICITY:
> No, this was years ago, but I think on it whenever I see him.

GLORIA:
> What you need is a good psychiatrist.

FELICITY:
> He wanted to kiss me. And I, of course, wanted to kiss him. I remember he smelled of straw. Wet straw. It had rained the night before and everything was damp. I'd fallen in the mud and he extended his hand to mine. I reached for it and he pulled me up into his arms. We stood there staring at each other for the longest time. God, how I wanted him.

GLORIA:
> Oh, please.

FELICITY:
> I stroked my rosary many a time that night I can tell you.

GLORIA:
> Felicity, please, there are some things I don't need to know.

FELICITY:
> Are you a lesbian?

GLORIA:
> What?

FELICITY:
> It's ok, you can tell me.

GLORIA:
> Who put that thought in your mind?

FELICITY:
> I wouldn't tell my father.

GLORIA:

> I am not a lesbian. Just because I hate men does not make me a lesbian.

FELICITY:

> Have you ever been in love?

GLORIA:

> I said I'm not a lesbian.

FELICITY:

> I mean in general.

GLORIA:

> I've seen too many wives pay for the sins of their husbands to ever want one of my own. "Oh but love" they cry "Sweet love. Precious love". Love isn't blind. She's stupid.

(Enter Jude playing guitar and singing)

JUDE:

> My love is such a flower
> I love to see her bloom
> So I give love my water
> And drown in her perfume

GLORIA:

> Oh, for the love of Nancy.

JUDE:

> My love is like...

GLORIA:

> That's enough. Stop it!

JUDE:
> What?

GLORIA:
> What did I tell you?

JUDE:
> You said you hated my piano. You didn't say anything
> about guitars.

GLORIA:
> How often do you want me to say it? I hate *you*.

JUDE:
> I'm sorry, you're right. It's the poor musician who blames
> his instrument.

GLORIA:
> Go away Jude.

JUDE:
> How about you, Felicity? Did you like the song?

FELICITY:
> Well, Jude, I...

GLORIA:
> You'll soon be a soprano if her father finds you here.

JUDE:
> The true artist lets no danger impede upon his muse.

GLORIA:
> Did you just use the word muse?

JUDE:

My instructor says I have a talent that defies description.

GLORIA:

Your instructor drinks. Heavily.

JUDE:

She says that one day I may be famous. That words and music have the capacity to transform the world.

GLORIA:

The ceasing of your verse is all the strides this world may ever hope to gain.

JUDE:

And then you'll wonder why you treated me so poorly.

GLORIA:

No, I'm pretty sure *that* I'll remember.

JUDE:

Let me at least finish it for you.

GLORIA:

Jude, your music makes me sick!

JUDE:

You haven't even heard the whole song.

GLORIA:

Who could stand it?

JUDE:

Hmmm, maybe this guitar is out of tune.

GLORIA:
>Jude, listen to me carefully. Jude! I don't love you. Whether you play the flute, the horn, the drums, the piano, or this guitar makes no difference to me. I don't love you. I will *never* love you. I would rather be raped by rabid cattle. If you were the last man on earth I would kill you for the meat. What makes you men think that we women are nothing more than ornaments to be strung upon your solitude? You're pathetic.

(Jude pauses for a moment and then takes up his song again with determination)

JUDE:
>My love is like an ocean
>As wide as wide can be

GLORIA:
>I'll see you this evening, Felicity.

JUDE:
>And when the waves are rollin'
>I'll not abandon thee.

>*(Gloria exits and Jude stops playing)*

FELICITY:
>I thought it rhymed very nicely, Jude.

JUDE:
>How I wish I had never laid eyes upon that woman. Or my heart could, by some other means, be given peace. She's made a dog of me - devoted cur that I am; fawning with tricks, docile and undignified. Quite content to renounce my pride for the slightest measure of kindness.

FELICITY:
> And has she shown you any?

JUDE:
> Not once.

FELICITY:
> So why do you pursue her?

JUDE:
> Isn't it obvious?

FELICITY:
> Not particularly.

JUDE:
> I'm a groveling idiot.

FELICITY: *(Hugging him)*
> Oh, Jude. Come here.

JUDE:
> I'm utterly hopeless.

FELICITY:
> Perhaps in time she'll reconsider.

JUDE:
> That's very kind of you to say. It's a blatant lie, but I appreciate it.

FELICITY:
> My pleasure.

(Enter Matthew carrying a large walking stick which he begins to use to strike Jude repeatedly)

MATTHEW:
> You let go of her, you *worm*! You filthy snake. Unhand my daughter!

JUDE:
> Hey! Ow! Stop it.

MATTHEW:
> You swine! You locust! You insect!

FELICITY:
> What are you doing? Stop it.

(Jude falls to the ground and curls up into the fetal position to protect himself)

JUDE:
> Somebody call him off of me!

FELICITY:
> Father, please, stop hitting him!

(Matthew pauses, exhausted)

MATTHEW:
> Oh, Felicity. I'm so ashamed.

JUDE:
> You should be.

(Matthew starts beating him again)

MATTHEW:
> I'll pluck out thy tongue, you serpent!

JUDE:
> I didn't *do* anything! I swear.

FELICITY:
> He's telling the truth.

(Matthew stops)

MATTHEW:
> You think I don't have eyes, Felicity?

FELICITY:
> You have no idea what you've seen here.

MATTHEW:
> Gloria told me. She told me I'd find him here. Strutting about like a randy peacock.

JUDE:
> I wasn't strutting! There was no strutting!

FELICITY:
> He didn't come here because of me.

MATTHEW:
> Or so he'd have you believe. These men are devious, Felicity. I know their kind. I know them all too well.

FELICITY:
> He's innocent.

MATTHEW:
> All men are guilty!

(Again Matthew begins to hit him, serving one blow on the beat of each of the following insults)

You're a spineless, soulless, foul-mouthed, sinner?

JUDE:
Foul-mouthed?

MATTHEW: *(Stops his assault)*
You're a miserable maggot!!!

FELICITY:
Leave him alone

(Jude manages to get to his feet and escape offstage)

MATTHEW: *(Breathing heavily)*
I think I've begun to let down my guard a bit in my old age.

FELICITY:
I'm beginning to think you're just getting meaner

MATTHEW:
Felicity!

FELICITY:
It's the truth isn't it?

MATTHEW:
When did you become so disrespectful? You see? Much depends upon the company you choose.

FELICITY:
I'm not allowed to choose anything.

MATTHEW:
Felicity, these men may seem virtuous to you, but they use that deception to steal your own. They would lead you

23

into hell but for no other reason than it pleases them to
do so.

FELICITY: *(Muttering)*
No wonder mother left us.

MATTHEW:
What did you say?

FELICITY:
Nothing. I'm sorry. Nevermind.

MATTHEW:
'Things were not always as they are today / The world was
once a happy place to play / But for one apple, on one
fateful day / Would all these cares and woes be swept
away.' Your mother wrote that.

FELICITY:
I know.

MATTHEW:
You mustn't fall to the same temptation.

FELICITY:
It doesn't seem as if I have a choice now does it? You're
always walking in my shadow.

MATTHEW:
Precisely. I'll not make the same mistake again.

FELICITY:
I'll be in my room. Will you at least call me when Gemini
arrives?

MATTHEW:
> Why?

FELICITY:
> His father was always kind to me. Why should I disrespect his son? We should invite him to dinner.

MATTHEW:
> That won't be necessary. He won't be staying with us for long. Go busy yourself.

FELICITY:
> Yes, father.

(Felicity exits)

MATTHEW:
> Poor child. Let not her sinful heart lead her astray, Lord. She's young. Have mercy.

(Matthew exits)

SCENE 3
Maverick's home

(There is a statue of a woman posed center-stage)

(Maverick and Gemini enter)

MAVERICK:
> What did I tell you, Gemini? Isn't she a beauty? Helen of Troy would pale by comparison. That face which launched a thousand ships would lose her suitors when the winds of this fair angel blew across their sails.

GEMINI:
> You're doing it again.

MAVERICK:
> What?

GEMINI:
> Breaking into song.

MAVERICK:
> I apologize.

GEMINI:
> She's very elegant.

MAVERICK:
> Elegant? Gemini, tea parties are elegant. Men would give their *lives* for this beautiful creature.

GEMINI:
> Lonely men, I'm sure.

MAVERICK:
Lonely men, indeed.

GEMINI:
She *is* beautiful.

MAVERICK:
We are all, are we not, fodder for worms? Each day brings us closer to their feast. Rotting away like fruit left out in the open air. But she leaves me feeling strangely immortal.

GEMINI:
We need to find you a real woman.

MAVERICK: *(sarcastically)*
Yes, that will solve everything.

(Jude enters)

JUDE:
Maverick! Thank God you're here.

MAVERICK:
What happened to you?

JUDE:
Old man Matthew.

MAVERICK: *(Laughing)*
Good Lord, what did you do?

JUDE:
I swear, nothing. It was just a case of mistaken identity. Gloria was visiting...

MAVERICK:
    Gloria? Again?

JUDE:
    Don't lecture me. I know. I know.

MAVERICK:
    She's a hellcat.

JUDE:
    Doesn't it look as if I know that? She told the old bastard
    that I was after his daughter.

MAVERICK: *(To Gemini)*
    Take note, my friend, for this shall soon be you.

GEMINI: *(Dryly Sarcastic)*
    Yes, I've heard all those awful stories of insane, old,
    crippled men destroying whole civilizations.

MAVERICK: *(Playing along)*
    He's far quicker than he might appear.

GEMINI:
    I'll have to be on my guard.

JUDE:
    He's like a lion, I'm telling you. He pounces before you
    even know he's there.

MAVERICK:
    A lion you say?

GEMINI: *(Smiling)*
    One without a mane.

JUDE:
> I'm telling you he's really quick. Like a crazed...cat of some sort. A tiger maybe. He beat me with a stick!

MAVERICK:
> Do tigers carry weapons?

GEMINI:
> Not that I'm aware of.

MAVERICK:
> We're dealing here with a very dangerous tiger.

JUDE:
> You mock me, but I'm telling you the man's insane. You should have heard him.

MAVERICK:
> A talking tiger now.

GEMINI:
> That's rare.

JUDE:
> The two of you can both go hang yourself!

(Jude turns to exit)

MAVERICK:
> Jude!

JUDE:
> I came to you for help.

MAVERICK:
> I'm sorry, we were just having a little fun.

JUDE:

At my expense. I get enough of that from her.

MAVERICK:

You're right. I apologize.

JUDE:

I want to teach her a lesson, Maverick.

MAVERICK:

What do you have in mind?

JUDE:

I know you fiddled around with chemistry in college. You couldn't have spent eight years there for nothing.

MAVERICK:

So?

JUDE:

Mix me up something to get Gloria to fall in love with me.

MAVERICK:

What?

JUDE:

Martin Rendall said he heard that you can turn metal into gold now or something.

MAVERICK:

That would be easier than concocting a potion to make Gloria love you.

JUDE:

I want her to suffer, Maverick. I want her to know my hell.

GEMINI:
Since when have you been mixing chemicals? I thought you were studying philosophy.

MAVERICK:
It was a hobby of sorts.

JUDE:
Please? Anything. I'll do anything.

MAVERICK: *(He retrieves the potion)*
Actually, I did come up with something during my freshman year. I was never able to duplicate it.

JUDE:
Does it work?

MAVERICK:
I'm not really sure.

JUDE:
What do you mean? Either it works or it doesn't.

MAVERICK:
I think it works too well. The faculty had to develop an antidote in the aftermath of the incidents. One fool even swore it brought his dead lover back to life. He wasn't happy.

JUDE:
Amazing.

MAVERICK:
Mind you, I don't believe a word of it. For the most part, people are idiots.

31

JUDE:
   I want it.

MAVERICK:
   You? What would you do with it? Teach the lady a lesson by making love to her?

JUDE:
   I'm through with her. I just want my revenge now.

MAVERICK:
   At least do me the courtesy of showing some respect for my intelligence. As soon as she is overcome with love for you, will you then be inspired with love again for her. It's all a vicious cycle.

JUDE:
   I'm only interested in true love.

MAVERICK:
   Nothing about love is true.

JUDE:
   Do you want to wager on it?

MAVERICK:
   It's too easy.

JUDE:
   If I take advantage of her affections, I'll give you whatever you want.

MAVERICK:
   Will you play a fool for me?

JUDE:
> A what?

MAVERICK:
> A fool. A jester. All dressed up like a clown of sorts.

JUDE:
> Agreed.

MAVERICK:
> For a month?

JUDE:
> You got it.

MAVERICK:
> Everywhere I go. Doing whatever I ask of you.

JUDE:
> Done.

MAVERICK:
> Then it's a bet

JUDE:
> Wait a minute. What are you going to stake against me?

MAVERICK:
> Nothing. I offer you the potion without a price. Now,
> whether you purchase it with foolishness is your decision.

JUDE:
> How will you know?

MAVERICK:
> I think we know each other well enough to be content with the honor system. Besides, no lover can hide his heart's affairs. You should take with you the antidote as well. Apply it the same as you would the potion, with one kiss to the lips of your intended.

(Maverick hands both the potion and its antidote to Jude)

JUDE:
> I hope it works.

MAVERICK:
> I'd like to see that myself.

(Jude exits)

GEMINI:
> I'm afraid I have to be going as well. Felicity awaits.

MAVERICK:
> And hope springs eternal.

GEMINI:
> You're really not much of an optimist are you?

MAVERICK:
> Gemini, when the world conforms to cheery thoughts and merry becomes each passing day, then may I consider myself deceased.

GEMINI:
> At least you could wish me luck.

MAVERICK:

> Good luck then, Gemini. And if by this wish may fortune decide to bless you, look upon it not with ease. For we are cursed with wishes more abundant and severe than these within us.

GEMINI:

> That's the spirit.

(Gemini exits)

(Maverick, reflecting, gazes upon the statue. He looks around the room to ensure that he is alone, and once satisfied, kisses the marble woman tenderly and exits)

SCENE 4
Felicity's garden

(Enter Matthew and Felicity)

MATTHEW:
>You will not see him. No!

FELICITY:
>Oh, please, father. Please? He could be leaving soon.

MATTHEW:
>I knew your thoughts for him were less than pure. Return to your room. You must fight this vile temptation.

FELICITY:
>I'm staying.

MATTHEW:
>Such insolence! Tell me, child, have I not provided for you? Have I not cared for your education and seen to your daily needs? And now, because the spark of lust has entered your heart, setting wildfire to your emotions, you would ignore that voice which has to this point shaped you? Disdaining wisdom that you might by freer choice thus let your spirit burn? It is hardly the stuff of angels, my dear.

FELICITY:
>Father...

MATTHEW:
>No arguments, Felicity. Now go!

FELICITY:
>But father, he's here.

MATTHEW:
>Off with you then.

FELICITY:
>Oh, please.

GEMINI:
>Hello, Felicity.

MATTHEW:
>You have no need to speak to her. It's me you've come to see. She was just leaving.

GEMINI:
>Let her stay. What I have to say concerns her as well.

MATTHEW:
>She has no concern which is not my own. Felicity, go.

FELICITY:
>Yes, father.

(Felicity exits)

GEMINI:
>She's old enough to make her own decisions.

MATTHEW:
>I don't recall asking your advice.

GEMINI:
>She's twenty years old.

MATTHEW:
>What is it you want, Gemini?

GEMINI:

    I'm here to see you repay your debt.

MATTHEW:

    You said that earlier. What debt?

GEMINI:

    The horse my father gave to Felicity.

MATTHEW:

    That was a gift.

GEMINI:

    Which you refused. I believe that's why you had this agreement drawn up. Is that not your signature?

MATTHEW:

    I more than repaid that debt with friendship.

GEMINI:

    I'm sorry, this document mentions no such arrangement.

MATTHEW: *(Reading)*

    You greedy swine. This note is worth more than a hundred horses.

GEMINI:

    Interest does add up over time.

MATTHEW:

    Your father would have never allowed...

GEMINI:

    My father is dead.

MATTHEW:
> And no doubt whirling in his grave.

GEMINI:
> I'm not here to argue with you.

MATTHEW:
> I certainly hope you are not here expecting to collect. I don't have this kind of money.

GEMINI:
> Perhaps we can arrange a bargain then?

MATTHEW:
> That's what you were hoping for all along, isn't it?

GEMINI:
> I'm always willing to compromise.

MATTHEW:
> I'm a simple man of simple means. I don't have much. The majority of my earnings have all gone to the church.

GEMINI:
> You do have a daughter.

(Pause)

MATTHEW: *(Matthew raises his cane)*
> Get out of here.

GEMINI:
> Hear me out.

MATTHEW:
> Get off my property!

GEMINI:
>I'm only suggesting...

MATTHEW:
>I know what you're suggesting, you lecherous slag!

>*(Matthew swings at Gemini and misses)*

GEMINI:
>I don't think you do.

MATTHEW:
>You wish that I should prostitute my daughter. You venereal, cankerous, maggot infested, polecat!

>*(Matthew swings again and misses)*

GEMINI:
>No, no, no, no, no, no, no. I only want to talk to her.

MATTHEW:
>I know what you want, beetle dung!

GEMINI:
>I want to talk. I only want to talk to her.

MATTHEW:
>Reprobate!

(Matthew charges and they both end up wrestling on the floor. Finally, Gemini emerges on top, holding Matthew down)

GEMINI:
>Relax! Will you just relax for a minute?

MATTHEW:
>I'll kill you! I swear, I'll kill you!

GEMINI:
>I only want to speak with her!

MATTHEW:
>I'll liquefy your brains!

GEMINI:
>I said I only want to speak with her!

MATTHEW:
>I'll pulverize your innards!

GEMINI:
>JUST GIVE ME A MINUTE TO SPEAK WITH HER!!

MATTHEW:
>I'll...what?

GEMINI:
>Talk. I just want to talk to her. In your presence, of course. But out of earshot. For as long as I see fit.

MATTHEW:
>No, it's a trick. You intend to steal her away from me.

GEMINI:
>I admit, I love her. If she doesn't love me, that'll be the end of it. But I need to know the truth. For that I need to speak to her.

MATTHEW:
>I won't allow it.

GEMINI:
>Then maybe she'll speak to me while you're away at prison. There are laws against defrauding an estate.

MATTHEW:
>That's ridiculous. You can't prove anything of the sort.

GEMINI:
>The courts do seem to recognize legal documents.

MATTHEW:
>You slick, cankerous, putrid, little troll.

GEMINI:
>I'm not afraid of you.

MATTHEW:
>You unrighteous, pernicious, decadent, little fag.

GEMINI:
>I would be very careful with my words.

>*(Pause)*

MATTHEW: *(Calmly)*
>So you wish merely to speak with her?

GEMINI: *(Suspicious)*
>Yes.

MATTHEW:
>And nothing more?

GEMINI:
>Nothing more than she might allow me.

MATTHEW:
> And if she allows you nothing?

GEMINI: *(Carefully beginning to let Matthew up)*
> Then I'll leave here for good.

MATTHEW:
> And the contract?

GEMINI:
> Will be yours to keep.

MATTHEW:
> No matter the outcome?

GEMINI:
> You have my word.

MATTHEW:
> May I have the chance to speak with her first?

GEMINI:
> Of course.

MATTHEW: *(Calling to her)*
> Felicity!

FELICITY: *(Offstage)*
> Coming, father.

MATTHEW: *(To Gemini)*
> Alone?

GEMINI:
> Of course. I'm sorry.

(Gemini moves away to the far end of the stage)

(Felicity rushes on)

MATTHEW:
> My, but you arrived here quickly.

FELICITY:
> I admit I was lingering a bit upon the fragrance of a rose.

MATTHEW:
> This gentleman is extorting me for the purposes of speaking with you. Under the circumstances, I'm afraid I must allow it. *(She smiles)* By your expression I see that this agrees with you. I suppose your generation finds blackmail to be an acceptable arrangement. However, I, too, can follow the letter of the law. While I must allow for your presence, he has placed no such value upon your participation. Therefore, you will speak not a word while in his company. Do you understand me? Not one word.

FELICITY:
> You want me to help you cheat him?

MATTHEW:
> Felicity.

FELICITY:
> I'm sorry, should we call it something else?

MATTHEW:
> I am not going to argue about it. If it's so important for you to speak with this man then by all means do so. But I will have neither wife nor daughter afterward.

FELICITY:
> You know that I've always been loyal to you.

MATTHEW:
> Then prove it to me now.

FELICITY:
> This isn't fair.

MATTHEW:
> You'll have to trust me, Felicity. I know what's best for you.

FELICITY:
> And when will you begin to trust me?

MATTHEW:
> This isn't the time for discussion. You know what I require of you. The decision is yours.

FELICITY:
> Yes, I know. Not a word.

MATTHEW:
> That's my girl.

(Felicity moves to meet Gemini downstage while Matthew remains apart, trying his best to listen in on their conversation while at the same time appearing nonchalant. It's apparent, however, that he cannot hear them)

GEMINI:
> Hello, Felicity...I'm sorry, I'm at a loss for words. I've waited so long for this moment and now I've forgotten what it was that I wanted to say. It feels strange to even be using words with you. As if I was speaking another

language. Up until now we shared silence as...I mean...Damn it, Felicity. The hell with all these stupid games. I'm through being so fearful of everything. We only live once, don't we? Carpe...something...Gather ye...Gather...ye rosebuds while ye have the chance...Oh, Christ, let's just run away together. I love you. And I think you love me, too. I hope you do anyway. We don't have to go far. I want to be with you. I want to smell you near me. I want to feel your hair on my face. I want to kiss you, Felicity. I've wanted to kiss you for so long now. Let's not be like all these other fools who love sheepishly or like some tame...Let's make love like wild animals. Let's really feel alive. We'll allow our passions to consume us like Tristan and Isolte or Romeo and Juliet. Only without all the dying, of course. We'll stop just short of dying. I mean...What do you say?

(Long pause in which Felicity struggles to keep silent)

What's the matter? Say something. Anything. Why won't you talk to me? *(He notices Felicity glance toward Matthew)* It's your father isn't it? He told you not to speak.

(Felicity seems to almost speak but instead gives up and bows her head in shame. Gemini reflects for a moment and then switches places with Felicity. The following he delivers in falsetto as if he were Felicity)

Gemini, I've waited so long to hear those words from you. I adore you. You are the most incredible man I've ever met. So strong. So handsome. So well put together. And smart, oh, don't get me started. Not a day goes by that I don't crave your company. To hell with my father. Meet me at midnight behind that huge oak on the hill that we both used to swing upon in better days. I'll steal away while my father sleeps.

(Gemini again switches places with Felicity and resumes his own identity)

Oh, it's too good to be true. Are you sure? If you mean to deceive me, please tell me now. Otherwise I'll meet you at midnight.

(Pause)

I knew that you would never mislead me. At midnight then, as you have requested. And if I may say, you have a wonderful way with words.

(Gemini returns to Matthew)

MATTHEW:
Are you satisfied?

GEMINI:
You cheated me. She didn't speak a word.

MATTHEW:
My apologies. She is a quiet one at times. However, if you might recall, I have held to my end of the bargain. I allowed you to speak with her.

GEMINI:
That's true.

MATTHEW:
May I have the contract then?

(Gemini hands him the contract and exits. Matthew crosses to Felicity and hugs her. She appears rather disoriented)

> My dear, you have made your old father quite happy. You should have seen his face. The fool actually thought he had outwitted me. Oh, look you not so grim, my child. There are better things out there for you than this stable-boy.

(Matthew and Felicity exit, she all the while looking back for Gemini)

SCENE 5
Maverick's dream

(Maverick enters carrying a bottle of wine)

MAVERICK:
>Oh, that the fates might pitch and strike this shape
>and throw this soul into constant turmoil,
>like the true lover burns amidst the flames,
>hardly seems a fortune to be fearful
>for one left numb to the coursing of his veins

(Statue enters)

STATUE:
>Hello, Maverick

MAVERICK:
>How do you know my name?

STATUE:
>You don't recognize me? Oh, is that wine? May I have
>some please? Oh, how I've missed the taste of wine.
>Among other things. You know, I've been celibate for
>almost two thousand years? I must admit, I rather
>enjoyed the first few hundred. Eternity though is far
>longer than you might expect.

MAVERICK:
>I imagine.

STATUE:
>Are you drinking or may I have the bottle?

MAVERICK:
>Please.

STATUE:
>A toast. To wine and music. May we soon be drunk with both.

MAVERICK:
>I'm sorry, I didn't bring any music.

(The Statue waves her hand and music is heard)

STATUE:
>Dreamers and the dead have many things in common. The primary being that all rules of order do not apply. This is really good wine.

MAVERICK:
>Can I ask you something?

STATUE:
>It's gone straight to my head.

MAVERICK:
>Am I dreaming?

STATUE:
>Of course, after two hundred years of abstinence I could get light-headed from a grape.

MAVERICK:
>Is this real?

STATUE:
>Do I seem any less real than, say, Mesopotamia? Or matter, for that matter? Isn't everything made up of energy? And what is energy, really? The universe is entirely an interpretation of the mind.

MAVERICK:
Why does that sound familiar?

STATUE:
I don't take credit for it. The thought was yours. After all, I'm a figment of *your* imagination.

MAVERICK:
You're quite a vivid one.

STATUE:
Why, thank you. I do try to keep up appearances.

MAVERICK:
Why are you here?

STATUE:
You have wine.

MAVERICK:
No, I mean, why are *both* of us here?

STATUE:
I'm afraid the secrets of one's dreams are all neatly woven together and one thread, loosened from that sacred weave would leave the whole fabric a limp and tattered web. A toast then, to dreams.

MAVERICK:
And the fools who dream them. Soon enough we shall all awake.

STATUE:
You're very cynical aren't you?

51

MAVERICK:
Do you know what I wish?

STATUE:
What?

MAVERICK:
I wish that I could be passionate about something.
Anything. I've always admired people with passion. Don
Quixote, for instance. He was an imbecile, but at least he
was passionate about it.

STATUE:
Why aren't you?

MAVERICK:
An imbecile?

STATUE:
Passionate.

MAVERICK:
Because it doesn't matter. Essentially, nothing really
matters. In the end. We create for ourselves a thousand
little diversions. We love. We laugh. We cry. For no
reason whatsoever. We hope. We dream. Why? All of it
comes to nothing in the end. We envision that our
existence counts for something. I mean, how egotistical.
We're nothing more than fleas if you think about it. We're
parasites with delusions of grandeur. Our greatest
achievements will sooner or later all end up as dust, but
we find that impossible to believe. We'd rather dream up
fantastic stories of life ever-after, eternal love, universal
truth, and other such nonsense. They're nothing more
than lies.

STATUE:
Like talking statues?

MAVERICK:
You see? Even I'm not immune to it. It's part of the human condition, I think.

STATUE:
Exactly. Come dance with me awhile.

MAVERICK:
I don't know how to dance.

STATUE:
This is a dream, remember? Everyone dances while they slumber.

(They come together and exit dancing)

SCENE 6
Felicity's garden

(Enter Gloria being pushed from behind by Felicity who cups a hand over her mouth)

FELICITY: *(Whispering)*
  Sshhhhhh. He'll hear you!

GLORIA:
  Good! Good! He should hear me.

FELICITY:
  He can't know anything about it.

GLORIA:
  Are you insane? Have you lost your mind? Is that it?

FELICITY:
  I only said I was considering it.

GLORIA:
  You'd consider going into the woods in the middle of the night to meet some guy that you've barely spoken with? This doesn't strike you as the least bit insane?

FELICITY:
  Be quiet! You'll wake my father.

GLORIA:
  God forbid you should be given a little sense. For all you know this guy could be an axe murderer.

FELICITY:
  Now who's being ridiculous?

GLORIA:

> Are you listening to me? He's named after an astrological sign for crying out loud. He can't be stable.

FELICITY:

> Gloria, I've spent my whole life listening to other people tell me what's best for me. I'm afraid that someday I won't even have my own opinion on the subject. So, in three hours I'm going up that hill to meet Gemini. If it's a mistake, then fine, it's a mistake. But at least it'll be my mistake.

GLORIA:

> Then let me go with you.

FELICITY:

> You can't.

> *(Jude enters)*

JUDE:

> What a surprise to find you ladies here.

GLORIA:

> What are you doing here, Jude? Go home. This is private property.

JUDE:

> No need to call out the dogs, Gloria. I'm here to say goodbye. You've made it clear that my feelings for you are unrequited. So be it.

GLORIA:

> Is this some kind of trick, Jude?

JUDE:

> No tricks. I just have one final request.

GLORIA:

>Don't threaten me, Jude. You're not man enough for suicide.

JUDE:

>I see that someone has a rather high opinion of themselves.

GLORIA:

>What do you want?

JUDE:

>A kiss. On the lips.

GLORIA:

>Are you nuts?

JUDE:

>Don't you want to be rid of me?

GLORIA:

>I'm not kissing you.

JUDE:

>A kiss is all I ask. One kiss to be rid of me forever.

GLORIA:

>I might be sooner freed from gravity.

JUDE:

>You have my word on it.

GLORIA:

>That's worth about a penny.

JUDE:
> It's worth a good deal more I can assure you.

GLORIA:
> How much more?

JUDE:
> What?

GLORIA:
> Five hundred pounds. If you go back on your word I want five hundred pounds.

JUDE:
> You want me to pay five hundred pounds to kiss you?

GLORIA:
> You won't have to pay it. Not as long as you never bother me again. Otherwise, I want cash.

JUDE:
> Agreed.

GLORIA:
> Felicity, you're a witness.

(Gloria hesitantly kisses Jude)

JUDE:
> Very well, Gloria. I only hope you don't regret your choice.

GLORIA: *(Stunned)*
> Good riddance.

(Jude exits)

FELICITY:
I think you encourage him sometimes.

GLORIA:
I do?

FELICITY:
Yes, I think you enjoy it. Why else would you agree to kiss him?

GLORIA:
I do.

FELICITY:
At least you might give him a chance.

GLORIA:
Oh, Felicity.

FELICITY:
I know. I know. All men are phagocytes.

GLORIA:
I've made a terrible mistake.

FELICITY:
What?

GLORIA:
You're right. You're right. I've made an awful, terrible mistake. I love him, Felicity. I've never been so sure about anything in all my life. Oh, God, I think I have a fever. I'm burning up. What have I done? I have to get him back.

FELICITY:
Jude?

GLORIA:

Yes, Jude. Didn't you just say so yourself? Hasn't it been obvious to everyone? I've been in love with him all along. I've just been fooling myself, Felicity. Deep down I've been yearning for him. But I've been playing hard to get. Toying with his emotions. Wallowing in my stubborn pride. And now he's left me for good.

FELICITY:

It's just a little sudden.

GLORIA: *(Growing inspired)*

I don't have time to discuss it with you. My love has sped, my heart has fled, I shall be dead if I find him not by morn. *(Snapping out of it)* Anyway, you get the idea.

(Gloria rushes out after Jude)

FELICITY: *(Inspired herself)*

The night is strange. It may bring together more lovers than are found in all of France. I can't wait until midnight. I'm coming for you Gemini.

(Felicity exits in a rush)

SCENE 7
Maverick's dream

(Maverick and the Statue enter dancing)

STATUE:
> You dance wonderfully.

MAVERICK:
> I've heard that in dreams blind men receive the gift of sight.

STATUE:
> I think I'd like some more wine.

(They stop dancing and Maverick pours her a glass of wine)

MAVERICK:
> Tell me something. Truthfully. What's going on here?

STATUE:
> I'm sorry. I can only answer those kinds of questions indirectly.

MAVERICK:
> Fine, then tell me indirectly why you're here?

STATUE:
> I have a message for you. It reads, 'The heart of a wise man resides in sorrow. The heart of a fool, with joy,'

MAVERICK:
> That's pretty indirect all right.

STATUE:
> I could tell you a story.

MAVERICK:
>It better be pretty short. Dreams don't last forever.

STATUE:
>Once upon a time there lived a pleasant old man who would spend his days at the local theatre. Though there were no performances on these days, he still sat in his seat and laughed and cheered and enjoyed himself thoroughly. Then, at night, he would return to his wife and family and was the most devoted family man. His friends, however, thought he must be insane to waste his time watching some imaginary performance up on the stage. So they cured him of his madness with a potion made of lye and the man saw the truth. The stage was bare and the actors had been nothing more than figments of his imagination. Fairly soon afterwards the man committed suicide. So you see, the wise man by wisdom made sane is oftentimes the fool.

MAVERICK:
>No, I think you could say he was a fool from the outset.

STATUE:
>You see, the gods, to prevent the tediousness of life, have proportioned thought and emotion accordingly. A pound of feeling to a single ounce of insight. You've reversed the process and now you're suffering for it.

MAVERICK:
>There are no gods. Not anymore.

STATUE:
>Perhaps not by name. But look around you. How do you explain such beauty?

MAVERICK:
>I don't know.

STATUE:
>Let's dance some more. While we still have time.

(They dance slowly, eventually ending in a position where Maverick is clinging to the statue's feet and the statue has returned to her usual posture. Maverick has awoken from his dream and the scene is now back in Maverick's home)

MAVERICK:
>What time is it? My god, it's still early. Oh, but this gentle ache is familiar. Indeed, my naked spirit, returning from the pleasures of cold, forbidden woods, has slipped again into her warm daycoat. This sheer and fragile garment laced of veins. I need some fresh air.

(He exits)

SCENE 8
The street

(Enter Jude quickly followed by Gloria)

JUDE:
 I told you. I gave you my word.

GLORIA:
 To me! You gave your word to me. Forget about it.

JUDE:
 Thank you. Goodnight.

GLORIA:
 No. No. No. No. No. No. Won't you stay with me for awhile?

JUDE:
 Why?

GLORIA:
 You could sing for me again.

JUDE:
 Don't toy with me. You hate my singing.

GLORIA:
 Where did you ever get that idea?

JUDE:
 I believe they were your exact words.

GLORIA:
 Oh, please. I was flirting.

JUDE:
> Flirting?

GLORIA:
> I didn't want you to think I was too easy of a catch. I was testing you.

JUDE:
> You loathe me. You said so yourself.

GLORIA:
> No.

JUDE:
> I hope you're having fun at my expense.

GLORIA:
> No, wait! How can I convince you?

JUDE:
> I'll have to think of something.

GLORIA: *(Coyly)*
> I may know a way.

JUDE: *(Falling under her spell)*
> You've never looked at me like that before.

GLORIA:
> That's funny. I can't seem to look at you any other way.

JUDE:
> Stop it.

GLORIA:
> I can't. I told you.

JUDE: *(Suddenly)*
>I should be going.

GLORIA:
>No, stay.

JUDE:
>You're mocking me! You've been mocking me from the very first day I ever laid eyes on you.

GLORIA:
>No, I'm not. Please. I'll prove it to you. How can I prove it to you?

JUDE:
>You can't

GLORIA:
>Please. I'll do anything.

JUDE:
>Well...

GLORIA:
>Yes? What?

JUDE:
>Fate would know the truth.

GLORIA:
>Fate?

JUDE:
>We'll flip a coin. You call it. Heads or tails?

GLORIA:
> I don't understand.

JUDE:
> It's simple. Have not all the great lovers through time been destined to be with one another?

GLORIA:
> I suppose so.

JUDE:
> And have they not all been faced with obstacles to their love?

GLORIA:
> I guess.

JUDE:
> And has fate not intervened in their behalf?

GLORIA:
> Yes.

JUDE:
> Then you have nothing to fear. Unless you're lying.

GLORIA:
> I'm not lying to you. I love you. I told you. I love you.

JUDE: *(He flips the coin)*
> Then call it in the air.

GLORIA:
> Heads.

JUDE: (*He catches it*)
>   It's heads.

GLORIA:
>   It's heads? It's heads? Oh my god, it's heads. You see?
>   You see, I told you.

JUDE:
>   I don't know what you're talking about.

GLORIA:
>   Fate decided. She knew I was telling the truth.

JUDE:
>   Whatever gave you that idea?

GLORIA:
>   It was heads. I called it.

JUDE:
>   Yes, to let your so called love be smeared by the
>   opportunity of chance. You would let a *coin* decide the
>   content of your heart? You might as well wager your soul
>   on a game show. You make me sick.

GLORIA:
>   No, wait!

>   *(Jude exits followed quickly by Gloria)*

SCENE 9
The woods

(Felicity enters dancing followed by Gemini. They both are in a partial state of dress)

FELICITY:
> I feel so alive. What a glorious night!

GEMINI:
> I agree. Glorious.

FELICITY:
> Did you hear me, father?

GEMINI:
> I think the world just heard you.

FELICITY:
> I'm here half-naked!

GEMINI:
> Sshhhhhh.

FELICITY:
> In the woods! *(Teasing)* With all the wild animals.

GEMINI:
> I think I've created a monster.

FELICITY:
> The stars! Oh, look how bright they are, Gemini. It's an omen. A sign that we were meant to be together.

GEMINI:
> I don't need a star to tell me that.

(He leans over to kiss her)

FELICITY:
>Oh, look, Gemini! A falling star.

GEMINI:
>Wish on it.

FELICITY:
>Should I?

GEMINI:
>Why not?

FELICITY: *(Closes her eyes)*
>Star light, star bright.

(Gemini joins her in reciting)

>The first star I see tonight. I wish I may. I wish I might. Have this wish I wish tonight.

GEMINI:
>I'll bet I know your wish.

FELICITY:
>I'll bet I never tell you.

GEMINI:
>To stay with me here forever.

FELICITY:
>My, someone has quite an ego.

GEMINI:
>That was my wish.

FELICITY:
> Then you've spoiled it by telling me. Now it won't come true.

GEMINI:
> I'm not all that superstitious.

FELICITY:
> My mother used to say that angels would whisper secrets to me while I slept. And to keep me quiet, they'd press their finger to my lip. And that's why I have this cleft below my nose.

GEMINI:
> Let's fly away somewhere. To Paris maybe.

FELICITY:
> That would be nice.

GEMINI:
> We could be married there.

FELICITY:
> Or Italy. Or Rome! How romantic.

GEMINI:
> Gather up your clothes. Let's get going.

FELICITY:
> Where?

GEMINI:
> To Rome. To Italy. To Paris. Why should we care? We'll be together.

FELICITY:
> You're joking, of course.

GEMINI:
> No I'm not joking. Let's go.

FELICITY:
> You mean elope?

GEMINI:
> Unless you have a better idea.

FELICITY:
> My father would be devastated.

GEMINI:
> He'll understand.

FELICITY:
> Gemini.

GEMINI:
> Eventually.

FELICITY:
> You know my father.

GEMINI:
> Yes, he's a bitter, uptight, twisted, old man who keeps his daughter chained at his side. He takes advantage of your kindness.

FELICITY:
> If I'm to marry anyone it will be with his consent.

71

GEMINI:
>So did you confide in him before you came to me tonight?

FELICITY:
>I didn't have any plans to run away with you at the time. He needs me, Gemini.

GEMINI:
>I need you more.

FELICITY:
>You don't understand. He wasn't always so...When my mother left us it changed him. You know he still cries over her? I see him sometimes in the kitchen looking at pictures. It nearly killed him when she left. And now you want me to do the same thing to him? I can't. I can't do it. I won't. Please, Gemini, just be patient. I know that sooner or later he's going to grow tired of this man that he's become and then everything will be different. Things will be as they were before.

GEMINI:
>What, when you were five?

FELICITY:
>I should be getting home. Will you walk with me?

GEMINI:
>Why are you making this so difficult?

FELICITY:
>You'll find that love is nothing more than friendship made to bear the worst.

GEMINI:
>Listen to me.

FELICITY:
Unless you wish to join me, we have nothing more to say.

GEMINI:
I've already left him a letter.

FELICITY:
What kind of letter?

GEMINI:
I had Jude deliver it for me. I told him to leave it on your doorstep.

FELICITY:
What did it say?

GEMINI:
How was I to know you wouldn't want to run off with me? I assumed that you loved me.

FELICITY:
Gemini, what did it say.

GEMINI:
I told him we were going off to get married.

FELICITY:
You what? Are you out of your mind? You left a letter like that for my father to find? What time is it? My God, it's almost morning. If he finds me gone and that letter on our doorstep...

(They exit in a hurry)

SCENE 10
The street

(Maverick enters in his robe and slippers)

GLORIA: *(Off)*
>Jude!

(Enter Jude followed by Gloria on her knees)

JUDE:
>Hello, Maverick. You're up rather early. Gloria, my love, meet my friend Maverick.

GLORIA:
>I heard you call me 'love.' You said, 'my love.' You can't deny it. You heard him didn't you?

JUDE:
>What terrible manners. For a moment there I had a sense of pity for you, though I see now why I can never call you 'love.' You're nothing but a slobbering dog. Get away! Go on!

GLORIA:
>No, please, Jude. Please. I was so overcome that you would even consider me at all. I'll be your dog if you wish. *(Getting on all fours)* See? I'm your devoted little spaniel.

JUDE:
>A spaniel? I doubt it. To call you spaniel would be to insult the breed. You appear more a nervous, little, hairless mutt.

MAVERICK:
>You're being a bit ruthless, don't you think?

JUDE:
> She has it coming to her.

GLORIA:
> Oh, I do. I do. I'm here on my knees to ask for your forgiveness, Jude. Please? I love you. I love you. I love you. I love you. I love you. I love you.

(Gloria continues her pleas while both she and Jude exit)

MATTHEW: *(Off)*
> Felicity! Felicity!

(Matthew enters frantically with letter in hand)

> Oh, Felicity. What's become of you? Oh, Lord, Felicity!

(Gemini and Felicity enter unnoticed by Matthew who sees Maverick for the first time)

> You! I know you! Where is he? Tell me where he is!

(The couple rush to hide themselves. Maverick does his best to keep Matthew's back to the pair)

MAVERICK:
> I'm sorry, who are you talking about?

MATTHEW:
> You know very well who I'm talking about. Your friend Gemini.

MAVERICK:
> I haven't seen him lately.

MATTHEW:

You're lying. I can always tell a liar when I see one.

MAVERICK:

Why are you looking for him?

MATTHEW:

He stole my daughter from her bed! And if I come to find that you had prior knowledge of it, I'll grind *your* innards into slop to feed my hogs.

MAVERICK:

Correct me if I'm wrong, but isn't that illegal?

MATTHEW:

It's a far better fate than Gemini shall receive. I'll hack his genitals and toss them to my dogs while he observes the feast. Then I'll loose those same hounds upon the wound until they've torn his groin to pieces.

MAVERICK:

Are you sure she's not in bed? You should check again. Maybe you only dreamed her gone.

MATTHEW:

It was no dream. If upon a bed she lays, that bed is not her own. And he who lies there with her I intend to wed upon a gravestone. Answer me. Where are they?

MAVERICK: (*Attempts to push Matthew back home*)

I have to warn you that anything you say can be held against you...

MATTHEW:

Unhand me! Perhaps you're trying to delay me? Is that it? You want to further their advantage?

MAVERICK:
> I'm only trying to prevent a Greek tragedy here.

MATTHEW:
> Unhand me, I said! Vengeance! I demand vengeance! Nothing else will satisfy. So it is written. So it shall be done! Vengeance is mine!

(Matthew runs off. Gemini and Felicity come out of hiding)

GEMINI:
> He's a lunatic.

MAVERICK:
> He does seem a tad upset.

GEMINI:
> He's a lunatic.

FELICITY:
> Why is he up so early? He never gets up before eight.

MAVERICK:
> Indigestion?

GEMINI:
> Now do you believe me? We should get far away from here while we still have the chance.

FELICITY:
> You can't run from everything.

GEMINI:
> What's that suppose to mean? Besides, that's easy for you to say. It's not *you* he intends to castrate.

FELICITY:
He doesn't mean it.

GEMINI:
He sounded pretty sincere to me.

FELICITY:
He's just ranting.

GEMINI:
He was foaming at the mouth! Maverick, help me out here. You have genitals. Explain to her how dearly you hold them.

MAVERICK:
It seems to me the solution is simple. We need to eliminate his desire to kill you.

GEMINI:
Have you any advice less obvious? I say we leave. Who needs this aggravation?

FELICITY:
If you love me like you say you do, you'll stay. It's important to me, Gemini. Isn't that enough? Maverick, you said something about a solution?

MAVERICK:
I know a drug that if it's taken carelessly will kill a person instantly. However, if it's administered in the correct proportion, brings about a state of paralysis very similar to death. The Incas used to use it to get closer to God, I guess.

FELICITY:
So we take it and my father finds us dead?

MAVERICK:
> When Romeo and Juliet were discovered dead, didn't that bring about the end of the feuds between their two families? What then would have been the scene, if by some miracle, those two lovers had been returned to them? Nothing but tears of reconciliation.

GEMINI:
> It'll never work.

MAVERICK:
> Do you have any better ideas?

GEMINI:
> What prevents him from hacking me up while I lay there sleeping?

MAVERICK:
> And you so optimistic.

FELICITY:
> Maverick will be there to watch over us.

MAVERICK:
> I wouldn't miss it for the world. I only wish you'd live to see it.

GEMINI:
> You don't exactly inspire confidence.

(They all exit)

SCENE 11
The street

(Jude enters followed by Gloria)

GLORIA:
> Jude? Jude? Jude?

JUDE:
> What?

GLORIA:
> Tell me again what I'm supposed to do?

JUDE:
> I've told you three times already.

GLORIA:
> My love for you consumes my thoughts and to the bone strips away all my other cares.

JUDE:
> If you wish to prove that love you'll do as my friend Maverick has suggested.

GLORIA:
> I've forgotten his words to me exactly.

JUDE:
> We expect to find Felicity's father here outside Gemini's home. Remember so far?

GLORIA:
> That part I do, yes.

JUDE:

And you, distraught, are going to meet up with him. No doubt he's going to wonder why you're here. So, now, what do you say?

GLORIA:

That Gemini and Felicity are dead.

JUDE:

Is that how you're going to say it? Just like that? He'll never believe you if you say it like that. You have to put some *emotion* into it.

GLORIA:

Well, they're not really dead.

JUDE:

I told Maverick you were hopeless. Of course they're not really dead, but we want Matthew to *think* so. But you have to *sell* it. You have to put some *tears* into it.

GLORIA:

I don't know if I can do that.

JUDE:

Well you'd better do it anyway. Here he comes. Drown him with a flood of tears or I swear I'll never love you. In fact, I'll do you one better. Convince the man he's lost a daughter and I pledge that I'll be yours.

(*Jude hides upstage. Matthew enters. Gloria stands bewildered*)

MATTHEW:

Oh, Gloria, you don't know how glad I am to see you. Felicity is missing from her bed. Do you know anything about it? Did she tell you of her plans?

(Pause while Gloria looks between Jude and Matthew)

GLORIA: *(begins to sob hysterically)*

Oh, Matthew! You poor, poor, poor, creature. You poor thing. What bitter news. How I envy you your ignorance. And how I pity you.

MATTHEW:

What, child? Tell me. What?

GLORIA:

Oh, pity, pity, pity. How distraught I am. See my tears?

MATTHEW:

I fear I'll soon be weeping with you. Tell me the truth, child. Your explanation can't be worse than this delay in knowing.

GLORIA:

It were better that you never knew. Go! Believe that she's abandoned you.

MATTHEW:

Gloria, tell me what's happened!

GLORIA:

She's dead. Your Felicity is dead. All gone. All gone. But you mustn't blame her. She did it out of grief. Grief that she could not please both the men she loves. You and Gemini. Forgive her. Forgive her.

MATTHEW:

Has she taken her own life? Where is he, Gloria? Tell me where he is. I shall sever him from his love as he has severed me from mine.

GLORIA:

They took their lives together. By poison. They lie in coffins at your estate.

MATTHEW:

Am I to be cheated of vengeance, too? Oh, Felicity. Felicity, my dear child.

GLORIA:

I can take you to her.

MATTHEW:

Nothing more remains of her. It was her spirit which made her dear to me. Escort me there! Deliver me to where her soul resides. In heaven or hell, I no longer care. Oh, Felicity. Felicity.

GLORIA:

I'm sorry, Matthew. I don't know what to say.

MATTHEW:

I may still have some satisfaction. Yes, a call for justice.

GLORIA:

What?

MATTHEW:

I can hear it. I can hear it again and again. Desecrate the corpse! Yes, let the wolves feed upon the scoundrel's body! And the birds tear upon his flesh. And the insects lay maggots in his liver.

GLORIA:
>On second thought, maybe we should just stay here for awhile.

MATTHEW:
>Felicity, I will avenge your death!

(Matthew rushes off. Jude emerges from his hiding place)

JUDE:
>I certainly hope Maverick knows what he's doing.

(Gloria rushes to Jude and kisses him passionately)

GLORIA:
>Oh, Jude.

JUDE:
>What are you doing?

GLORIA:
>I'm celebrating. I have you now forever.

JUDE:
>I hardly think so.

GLORIA:
>But you said if I convinced the man. I convinced him. He left intent to violate the body. Do you doubt that I convinced him?

JUDE:
>Not at all.

GLORIA:
>Then why would you go back against your word?

JUDE:

> I made that promise to another woman. A woman that I thought I knew. Not this deceitful liar that stands here now. You're far too accomplished for me to ever trust you. How might I depend upon a thing you say? Words roll so smoothly off your tongue regardless of the truth in them.

GLORIA:

> You told me to do it.

JUDE:

> No, I told you to show distress and tell him of the news. I made no mention of the reasons for her suicide. You made that up yourself. I applaud you for it actually. It was a stroke of genius. Though not an attribute one looks for in a wife.

(She falls to her knees)

GLORIA:

> I can't take this any longer. I see now why lovers kill themselves so often. It's out of weariness isn't it? You see? This is why I've stayed so far away from love. It's nothing but a disease. A disease where the illness is the remedy. Love should be illegal. It should be a crime. Though no punishment worse than that already afflicted. If you won't love me, Jude, then I don't want to live. Goodbye.

JUDE:

> Wait, what are you doing?

GLORIA:

> I won't bother you anymore.

JUDE:
> You're willing to die for me?

GLORIA:
> You'll forget me soon enough.

JUDE:
> No, I don't want you to kill yourself. I only wanted you to suffer a little is all. I love you.

GLORIA:
> You wanted me to suffer?

JUDE: *(Sheepish)*
> Well, when you put it like *that* it sounds...

GLORIA:
> You're just trying to be kind. It's obvious that you don't love me. Though it was sweet of you to try.

JUDE:
> Listen, just wait a bit. Come with me.

GLORIA:
> Please, I'd like to get this over with.

JUDE:
> I have a better solution. If it doesn't work you can always kill yourself later.

(They exit)

SCENE 12
Maverick's House

(Enter Maverick, Felicity, and Gemini who is soiled from top to bottom)

MAVERICK:
>I swear I'll explain everything.

FELICITY:
>Just tell us if he's dead, Maverick.

MAVERICK:
>He's not dead, though he did take a rather slight bump to the head.

GEMINI:
>Not slight enough if you ask me.

MAVERICK:
>He's sedated now.

FELICITY:
>What happened?

MAVERICK:
>It was quite a scene, believe me. The whole thing went haywire from the start.

GEMINI:
>What happened to my clothes?

MAVERICK:
>That story is a longer one. Suffice it to say that everything turned out well in the end.

GEMINI:
I smell like the intestine of a cow's belly.

MAVERICK:
True.

GEMINI:
And why am I all battered up? You were supposed to watch over this whole thing.

MAVERICK:
I did. I tried. I wasn't expecting the response. He was a raving lunatic. He came to the house riding a white horse, naked as the day he was born, wearing a thorny wreath upon his head. I can't get the image out of my mind. At the time he seemed calm, but when I greeted him, he screamed, 'the apocalypse is now!' Then he leapt from the horse screaming obscenities, throwing punches and kicking at my knees. 'Hell is empty' he cried, 'for all the fiends are here!'

FELICITY:
Oh, my.

MAVERICK:
Then, just as suddenly, he went silent. He saw Felicity there in her coffin and he leaned over her and cried and cried until I was almost ready to call off the whole thing out of pity for him. But then he broke into a rage again and before I knew it he struck me in the head and I was lying on the floor.

GEMINI:
You let an old man knock you out?

MAVERICK:
I wasn't expecting it.

GEMINI:
He flattened you?

MAVERICK:
It could have happened to anyone. I wasn't expecting it.

GEMINI:
Well, I wasn't exactly expecting to wake up smelling like a stable horse.

MAVERICK:
Yes, would you mind standing upwind a bit?

FELICITY:
That's enough you two. Stop it.

MAVERICK:
Anyway, I was knocked unconscious for a little while. Not long, I'm sure. But enough that he escaped together with you both. Felicity slung over his lap and Gemini...behind.

FELICITY:
Behind?

GEMINI:
You mean slung over the horse's ass?

MAVERICK:
No, dragging behind the horse from a rope.

GEMINI:
What?

MAVERICK:
I didn't really have a choice in the matter.

GEMINI:
He could have killed me.

MAVERICK:
Relax. To him, you were dead already. And not many people have ever drowned in cow manure. I caught up with you pretty quickly.

FELICITY:
Where was he taking us?

MAVERICK:
As near as I can figure, he intended to feed Gemini to the wolves.

FELICITY:
Wolves? There are no wolves around her.

MAVERICK:
He wasn't exactly in his right mind. When I finally caught up, he mistook me for the devil.

GEMINI:
I told you this wouldn't work.

MAVERICK:
So, I thought it couldn't hurt. I started gnashing my teeth and calling him all sorts of names. Telling him that I intended to take him with me into hell and all the tortures he would endure there. Before I knew it, he'd wet himself. Then he turned quickly to run, but knocked himself cold on an overhanging branch. That's when I gathered all three of you together and brought you to my house. I

sedated him and tied him to a chair in the other room while we figure out what we're going to do.

GEMINI:
We're never going to be rid of him.

FELICITY:
He thought you were the devil?

MAVERICK:
It was dark. He was insane.

FELICITY:
Would you care to play that role again?

MAVERICK:
What do you have in mind?

FELICITY:
I was thinking that a journey into hell might not be a bad idea.

GEMINI:
What?

FELICITY:
Why not?

GEMINI:
Because. It's ridiculous.

FELICITY:
You just follow my lead and try not to say anything. Both of you go bring him here.

(Gemini and Maverick exit and return shortly carrying Matthew who's asleep and tied to a chair. Maverick is now carrying a black blanket)

MAVERICK: *(Holding up the blanket)*
Do you like it? A devil's cape.

FELICITY:
Quiet. We don't want to wake him.

MAVERICK:
No worry there. I have him pretty well sedated.

FELICITY:
We'll need to dim the lights. Do you have any candles?

MAVERICK:
In the kitchen.

GEMINI:
I'll get them.

(Gemini exits)

FELICITY:
I need three.

MAVERICK:
I'll get the lights.

(Maverick exits. Gemini quickly returns with three candles and some wooden matches. Felicity lights the candles and places them around Matthew. The lights dim and Maverick enters again)

FELICITY:
Are we ready then? Ok, wake him up, Maverick.

MAVERICK:
I think Gemini should have the honors.

GEMINI:
Why me?

MAVERICK:
Why not you?

FELICITY:
Fine, Gemini, you do it. Maverick, tell him what to do.

GEMINI:
No, wait a minute. I don't trust him. This doesn't sound right.

MAVERICK:
All you have to do is kiss him on the lips.

GEMINI:
You see?

MAVERICK:
With this potion.

GEMINI:
I told you.

FELICITY:
Do it, Gemini.

GEMINI:
What? Felicity!

FELICITY:
>How devoted are you?

GEMINI:
>Oh, no you don't. You can't keep throwing that in my face. He's your father. You kiss him.

FELICITY:
>It would show me how deeply you care. Not only for me, but for my family.

GEMINI: *(Taking the potion from Maverick)*
>Oh for the love of...

MAVERICK:
>I've heard that the father should kiss the bride but this...

GEMINI:
>Shut up.

(Gemini rubs the potion on his lips and hesitantly kisses Matthew who immediately awakens)

MATTHEW:
>Villains! Villains! I'll be revenged upon you all!

MAVERICK:
>Silence you overweening minnow! Marsupial of a lowly birth. Show more respect you canker. Thou bottom feeder. Thou Lord of lint. Nay, lord of vomit. Thou excrement!

GEMINI: *(Whispering)*
>Don't overdo it.

MAVERICK:
See thy daughter here? In company now with other lusty youth who also lost their souls to passion. They whose favors now are nightly violated to signify their lives which they let fly wasted.

MATTHEW:
Felicity? Oh, Felicity. Are we both dead now? And in hell? Oh, I warned you, child. I warned you.

MAVERICK:
Silence I say. Who are you to admonish her? She holds a higher place in hell than thee! You centipede. You weevil. Louse. Tick. Chigger.

GEMINI: *(Whispering)*
Maverick, enough.

FELICITY:
Sir, may I speak to my father alone?

MATTHEW:
Felicity.

MAVERICK:
What? Again you cross me, caterpillar? Must I bait my hook with thy tongue, you worm?

FELICITY:
Please, sir, it won't take long.

MAVERICK:
Very well. Be done with it.

(Maverick and Gemini move away. Felicity embraces Matthew)

95

MATTHEW:
> If only I were untied, my child.

FELICITY:
> Listen to me. You must repent. There still may be hope for you. For us both. I'm told the Lord sometimes will hear the cries of true contrition and will deliver those souls from here.

MATTHEW:
> But I've committed no sin. No sin but to love you with all my heart. If the Lord should wish to punish me for that...

FELICITY:
> The Lord has willed that I return to life having spent my time here in purgatory.

MATTHEW:
> The dead may return?

FELICITY:
> If it please God. Gemini is to go with me. We're to be married.

MATTHEW:
> I won't allow it! Never. I tell you I forbid it!

(Maverick and Gemini approach)

MAVERICK:
> Raise thy voice again, you pig, and I shall have you porked.

FELICITY:
> Please, Father. This is divine intervention. It's His will that we be married.

MATTHEW:

No. No. No. It's the work of this devil! This reptile!

MAVERICK:

Be wary of thy tongue, for I enforce the wrath of God. The executioner of his divine justice am I. Thou hedgehog. Crustacean. Snail. Clam. Scorpion!

MATTHEW:

Oh, Lord, let this be a dream.

MAVERICK:

'Tis no dream, frecklepuss. 'Tis a nightmare.

MATTHEW:

I will repent, my Lord. I will repent.

MAVERICK: *(Mocking)*

I will repent. I will repent. Too late for you, junglerot. You're damned.

MATTHEW:

For what sin, I beg you? Tell me. What sin?

MAVERICK:

Would you have me name it? There are so many. Namely for the sin of suffocation.

MATTHEW:

I've never heard of that.

MAVERICK:

Nevertheless.

MATTHEW:

> I object! Cite a precedent. My conduct is beyond reproach according to the law of God as it is written. I ask you. Cite a precedent.

MAVERICK:

> Suffocator, your lawyering will only make your punishment more severe. Lawyers here are tongue-plucked. However, if you wish to plead your case, let it be known that thy own daughter is a witness for the prosecution.

MATTHEW:

> Felicity? That's ridiculous.

MAVERICK:

> Did you not restrain her from every natural impulse?

MATTHEW:

> Of course. Of course. Is she an animal?

MAVERICK:

> Is she a stone? You'd have her cloistered if you could. Sent back to live within another time. Let it be known that God abhors a nun. You made of her mother an outcast, too. You killed her horse. You stole her childhood. You allowed her no contact with anyone of the opposite sex. And why? Because you're afraid. A sniveling, cowardly...

MATTHEW:

> Now see hear...

MAVERICK:

> Silence, I say! You are charged with suffocation. Thy penance shall begin immediately. Gemini, take him away

and whip him for your pains. A lash for every moment
this man kept the two of you apart.

MATTHEW:

If I knew that these were sins I'd have never committed
them.

GEMINI:

With pleasure.

MAVERICK: *(To Gemini)*

Take him to the cellar. And don't be too hard on him.

(Gemini drags the chair and Matthew off)

FELICITY:

Where's he taking him?

MAVERICK:

My cellar. If there were a hell, I image it would look very
similar. I need to get down there and clean one of these
days. I'll send Gemini over when he's finished and I'll
take it from there. It'll be kind of fun. You two have a
good time.

FELICITY:

How stubborn is he do you think? How long are we going
to be forced to keep him here?

*(Maverick is heard offstage wailing and begging with every
blow of the lash)*

MAVERICK:

Oh, not very long I don't think. If he's not already
repented, I'm sure he will by morning.

FELICITY:
> Gemini better not hurt him.

MAVERICK:
> We don't want to make it too easy on him. Anyway, it's not a real whip. His mind is creating most of his suffering. Now, go get some sleep.

FELICITY:
> Ok, goodnight, Maverick.

MAVERICK:
> Goodnight.

(They both exit separately)

SCENE 13
Felicity's garden

(Jude and Gloria enter)

GLORIA:
What are we doing here?

JUDE:
It'll be like you never left.

GLORIA:
What will?

JUDE:
Nevermind. It doesn't matter.

GLORIA:
What are you talking about, Jude?

JUDE: *(applying the antidote to his lips)*
I'm an idiot, Gloria. A fool. You deserve much better. I just want you to know that I never meant to hurt you. That's not true. I guess I did. But I won't anymore. I'm sorry. May I kiss you?

GLORIA:
Of course.

(He kisses her)

JUDE:
Goodbye, Gloria.

(Gloria has emerged from the kiss in a daze and comes to her senses quickly after Jude exits)

GLORIA:
> Felicity? Where'd you go? Felicity? That's strange. She
> was just here. Wasn't she? Or did I fall asleep? Good
> Lord, what a dream. What a nightmare! How long have I
> been sleeping? She must have gone to meet...Oh my God!
> My dream. Felicity dies in my dream. It was a
> premonition. My dream was a premonition. Oh my God!
> Felicity!

> *(She exits in a rush)*

SCENE 14
Maverick's cellar

(Matthew sits tied to his chair in the middle of the room. Maverick enters)

MATTHEW:
> Pardon me, sir. I'm wondering if there will be food here. Who would have guessed that hunger was a trait of death?

MAVERICK:
> You'll be fed when I'm ready to feed you.

MATTHEW:
> May I ask a question? Are you the devil?

MAVERICK:
> I'm his watchman. In purgatory, they call me Corsica.

MATTHEW:
> Is this damnation or purgatory.

MAVERICK:
> That's up to you, isn't it?

MATTHEW:
> May I have a drink of water?

MAVERICK:
> The only food and drink that you'll receive will be whatever is so offered in your name at church. Unfortunately, you've only had one visitor. Your daughter. She's brought you this.

(Maverick produces a cup of water and a loaf of bread from the table behind Matthew)

MATTHEW:

God bless that child. She, who has every reason to hate me, instead offers only charity. *(He tastes the food)* Damn her! What is this slop?

MAVERICK:

Water and bread. Probably flavored with mold and bitters. Two spices, I imagine, with which you're familiar.

MATTHEW:

Not at all! I'm not familiar with them at all.

MAVERICK:

You find the food unacceptable then?

MATTHEW:

Absolutely.

MAVERICK:

You should consider yourself fortunate. Think how edible might be a fornicator's meal. All those fluids and excretions. It's really quite disgusting. Or how sparse the dinner of a glutton. Or upon who's flesh dines the murderer. And you complain of a little bitterness?

MATTHEW:

Oh, this is horrible. If only I hadn't been such a tyrant.

MAVERICK:

I suppose I could plead your case before his Excellency the devil. He is cruel, but fair. He might grant you a pardon.

MATTHEW:
> I would be most grateful. I don't think I can endure anymore.

MAVERICK:
> Here he comes now. I'll petition him. But whatever you do, don't look back at him. He'll view it as contempt and could increase your punishment tenfold.

MATTHEW:
> Yes. Yes. I understand. Thank you.

> *(The scene is played out entirely behind Matthew)*

MAVERICK: (He alternates using the *voice of the devil* and that of the watchman)
> My Lord? My Lord? A moment, please? *What sayeth thou watchman? And whyfor doth this ringworm remain here in luxury? Did I not commend his flesh be peeled at once?* You did, my Lord. And I in all humility intend to carry out the deed. *What delays you then?* A motion, my Lord. An appeal for justice. *In justice do I intend to have him peeled.*

> *(To Matthew)*

> What exactly is your motion?

MATTHEW:
> What?

MAVERICK:
> What have you to say in your defense?

MATTHEW:
> That I am innocent.

MAVERICK:

> No. No. No. Do you think he's an idiot? You're only going to make him angry.

MATTHEW:

> But I'm innocent of the charges brought against me. A tyrant I may be, but suffocation? I've never even heard of such a sin.

MAVERICK:

> Sir, I contend that the accused is innocent by virtue of ignorance. *Ignorance before the law is no excuse. Have him flayed at once.* But, sir, there is precedence. Was Cain charged with murder when death had not yet been established as the norm? *Yes, he was.* He was? *Yes.* When did that happen?

MATTHEW:

> You're not helping.

MAVERICK:

> You need to fight the urge to face him.

MATTHEW:

> But I didn't plead ignorance. I pleaded innocence.

MAVERICK:

> *You dare interrupt these proceedings, maggot?* Straight ahead, man. Don't look backwards. *What sayest thou then? Speak! Teacheth me the ways of the universe thou wise and learned bedbug! Speak, I say!*

MATTHEW:

> Nothing, sir. Nothing. I think I've seen the error in my ways now and I'm intent to make amends. I've changed. I have. Please return me to my daughter.

MAVERICK:

> *Do you think me a simpleton? How often do you think I've heard those cries before? 'Oh, mercy! Mercy!' Those who dwell down within the deepest, darkest regions of my incinerator, each and every day, renounce their ways and vow to start anew. How many do you think are actually capable of it? None. Not a one. And these are souls that suffer greatly. Yet, they would rather choose to suffer than truly amend their character. How then might I believe you to be the first? You've yet to really suffer the tortures of hell. Take him from my sight, Corsica. And if he should even once complain of these accommodations as though he were undeserving, cast him in the pit of darkness, there to remain forevermore.*

Yes, my Lord.

(Pause)

He's gone.

MATTHEW:

I smelled the brimstone on his breath.

MAVERICK:

He has quite a temper. You would do best to listen. But don't lose hope. You're not yet dammed to hell. Let's go now. It's time for your ice water bath.

MATTHEW:

A bath in ice water?

MAVERICK:

I'm sorry. Do you have a complaint? Should I take it up with his Lordship?

MATTHEW:

> No. No. It sounds lovely. I've always enjoyed a cold bath. There's nothing quite like hypothermia to wake you up in the morning.

MAVERICK:

> Great. Then you're going to love where you'll be sleeping tonight.

MATTHEW:

> Anywhere is fine. I could make a pillow of a pile of rocks.

MAVERICK:

> Actually, you might do better to stay awake. This is a good time for some introspection.

MATTHEW:

> Well, sleeping is overrated anyway.

(Maverick escorts Matthew Off)

SCENE 15
Felicity's garden

(Enter Gemini and Felicity, arm in arm)

FELICITY:
> It's so peaceful here. There's no fear my father may be lurking around the corner. But I suppose it's only momentary, isn't it? Sooner or later we're going to have to let him out of there. What if it doesn't work? Or what if it's only temporary? Still, I miss him. Do you find that strange?

GEMINI:
> Yes. I do.

(Gloria enters and leaps upon Gemini's back and begins to struggle with him)

GLORIA:
> I knew it! I knew it! Felicity, run!

FELICITY:
> Gloria, have you gone insane?

GLORIA:
> I'll hold him. Run away!

GEMINI:
> Stop it!

FELICITY:
> Gloria, let go of him.

(Felicity pulls Gloria off of Gemini)

GLORIA:
> Felicity, you're in danger here.

GEMINI:
> Is everyone you know a lunatic?

GLORIA:
> Come on. You want a piece of me?

GEMINI:
> I'm not going to fight a woman.

GLORIA:
> All the better.

(Gloria jabs and connects with Gemini's jaw several times)

GEMINI:
> Did you see that? She just hit me! My lip is bloody!

(Felicity struggles to put herself between the two)

FELICITY:
> Gloria, this is ridiculous.

GEMINI:
> I'm bleeding!

GLORIA:
> I won't stop at your lip either.

(Gloria knees Gemini in the groin)

FELICITY:
> What's gotten into you? Have you lost your mind?

GLORIA:
> He intends to murder you. Ask him.

GEMINI:
> What are you talking about?

FELICITY:
> Gloria, I think you're just tired. You should go to bed.

GLORIA:
> I've just awoken. I think your boyfriend here might have tried to poison me or something. But it didn't work, did it?

GEMINI:
> What?

FELICITY:
> You've been up for hours. All night, in fact. We saw you only this morning with Jude and you told me so yourself.

GLORIA:
> That's ridiculous. Why would I be with Jude?

FELICITY:
> You poor thing. You're too tired to even remember.

GLORIA:
> Don't patronize me.

FELICITY:
> Then do you remember how you left me here a few days ago to chase after Jude? You claimed you loved him desperately. Then we met you clutching at his heel, remember? You told me that he was your everlasting

111

Bunny-bear. And then we used you both in a trick against my father. Sound familiar?

GLORIA: *(beginning to recall her memory of the evening)*
Was I on my knees begging Jude's forgiveness?

FELICITY:
In a way. More precisely you were singing his praises. First you called him, 'a man without compare, a faultless man.' Then I believe you referred to him in confidence as, 'that sweet-bottomed Jude.'

GLORIA:
How do you know my dream, Felicity?

FELICITY:
Because it happened. It was real. Or else we all were dreaming.

GLORIA:
You mean to say that Jude and I were...We were both...That I was...Did I then kiss him, too? In company? Oh, hell! How can I ever show my face again? The gossip, Felicity. I can hear them now. This is a small town. Everyone will know. They'll call me sister and speak to me of pigeons and turtledoves.

FELICITY:
Maybe I should take you home.

GLORIA:
And my reputation, Felicity. They'll stand outside my home and say, 'Look there in the window. Isn't that the mistress of supplication? The madam of hypocrisy? The dame of love?

FELICITY:
> It'll be ok.

GLORIA:
> You'll tell them, won't you? That I'm not really such a marshmallow. You'll tell them, right? Tell the children?

FELICITY:
> Whose children?

GLORIA:
> All of them?

FELICITY:
> Let's get you home.

(Felicity helps Gloria offstage as the three exit)

SCENE 16
Maverick's cellar

(Matthew sits sleeping in his chair as Maverick enters)

MATTHEW:
Who's there? Is that you, Corsica?

MAVERICK:
Yes, I have some visitors here for you. Angels from heaven. But first you need to wear this blindfold. Be careful you don't peek beneath it. The sight of them while you're still a living prisoner in hell will doom you to this place forever.

(Maverick begins to secure the blindfold over Matthew's face)

MATTHEW:
I'll close my eyes just to be sure. Angels from heaven? Dare I hope to be released from this place? Not that I'm complaining.

(Maverick finishes the task and Gemini and Felicity enter)

FELICITY:
Dear Matthew, we are messengers of the Lord.

GEMINI:
We bring you news.

MATTHEW:
Your voice. You sound just like my daughter.

FELICITY:
It's no wonder. It happens all the time. I'm often mistaken for a daughter or sister or lover or wife. We

angels possess those same qualities which men and women favor in their affections.

MATTHEW:
I miss her terribly. It's been nearly a month on earth I'm told.

GEMINI: *(trying his best to completely disguise his voice)*
The news we bring concerns your daughter.

MATTHEW:
I'm sorry, angel, but your voice is difficult for me to understand.

GEMINI:
You have to get used to it.

FELICITY:
Your daughter's to be married.

MATTHEW:
She told me.

FELICITY:
It is in her prayers that you attend the ceremony.

MAVERICK:
Why? What am I to her?

FELICITY:
Her father.

MATTHEW:
I'm nothing but a stranger to her. And to myself. She calls me father and I am the man who named her and was present at her birth. Who lifted her into his arms. She

smiled at me then and I was overcome with tears. How must she think of me now?

FELICITY:

She adores you, sir. You surrendered your happiness for her.

MATTHEW:

I sacrificed nothing. She was my daughter. I have no happiness in all the world to equal my love for her. To give my life is nothing. I wish I could bestow something of worth.

FELICITY:

Then come to her wedding, Matthew. It would be the perfect gift.

MATTHEW:

May I? I would love to see her happy. To see her smile again.

FELICITY:

Very well. The Lord has granted you a pardon on the behalf of your daughter. It will expire at midnight on the day of her wedding. Unless the Lord should choose to make it a permanent reprieve.

MATTHEW:

Permanent? You mean I could leave here for good?

FELICITY:

Of course, that would depend on how you choose to spend your future.

MATTHEW:

How will I know if the Lord should make it permanent?

FELICITY:
> You'll hear the bells of Saint Mary's cathedral chime. At midnight.

MATTHEW:
> From the condemned church? They haven't rung in decades.

FELICITY:
> Yes, it would be a miracle. Corsica, return this soul to earth.

> *(Maverick applies a potion and Matthew is asleep)*

> Ok, we need to put him back where he first fell in the forest.

MAVERICK:
> I have it all arranged. Jude's going to ring the bells at midnight.

FELICITY:
> Jude? Are you sure that's a good idea? We need this to be flawless.

MAVERICK:
> Don't worry.

FELICITY:
> Are you sure the bells still work?

MAVERICK:
> I said, don't worry. I have it all under control.

GEMINI:
> Weren't those the last words of Custer?
> > *(They exit carrying Matthew)*

SCENE 17
The woods

(Matthew, sleeping center stage, awakens)

MATTHEW:
> Hallelujah! I'm alive. I'm alive! I won't forget you for this, Lord. I won't forget. I promise. Oh, smell the forest. The birds. The bees. Oh, springtime!

(Jude enters dressed as a king's fool)

JUDE: *(Cautiously)*
> Aren't you Felicity's father?

MATTHEW:
> I am, my boy. I am, indeed.

JUDE:
> Someone told me you were dead.

MATTHEW:
> Resurrected, my boy. Resurrected!

JUDE:
> I was just on my way to your daughter's wedding.

MATTHEW:
> Is it a costume wedding?

JUDE:
> I'm a fool.

MATTHEW:
> Why, so am I. Are we required to be in special outfits?

JUDE:
> No, I lost a bet. It's a long story. Do you want to walk with me?

MATTHEW:
> Lead the way, my boy.

JUDE:
> You're not going to hit me again, are you?

MATTHEW:
> Hit you? Why, of course not. I'm a new man. An absolutely new man. Are you not a musician of sorts?

JUDE:
> I used to play a bit. I've abandoned it.

MATTHEW:
> Whatever for?

JUDE:
> I don't have the talent.

MATTHEW: *(Warmly)*
> This earth would be quite a silent place if only those with talent were allowed to play. It's my daughter's wedding day. I'd love if you would entertain us.

JUDE:
> If you say so.

MATTHEW:
> With Felicity's approval, of course.

(They exit)

SCENE 18
Felicity's garden

(Enter Gemini and Felicity)

FELICITY:
The bride isn't supposed to be seen before the wedding.

GEMINI:
That's just some superstition.

(Enter Gloria)

GLORIA:
Matthew is coming.

FELICITY:
Alone?

GLORIA:
No, Jude is with him.

FELICITY:
Does he seem angry at all?

GLORIA:
Hardly. The two of them are skipping like little school girls.

FELICITY:
Are you kidding?

(Enter Jude and Matthew arm in arm, singing)

MATTHEW:

> My child! My child. My child. My child. Have you grown even *more* beautiful? It hardly seems fair that you should hold in trust so much of all the world's magnificence. Look at you. How unjust of me to hide you away from everyone. The world's a better place that you are in it. Forgive me?

FELICITY:

> I do. Of course, I do.

MATTHEW:

> Where's your groom? *(To Gemini)* Son, I hope you'll make her happy. For no one in this world deserves it more than she. I wish for the two of you to lead a blissful, long, and happy life.

GEMINI:

> I intend to spend the rest of my days trying to be worthy of her.

MATTHEW:

> Well spoken, my boy. Very well spoken. Well, what are we waiting for? There's a wedding at hand isn't there? What are we all doing standing here?

JUDE:

> After you.

MATTHEW:

> I won't hear of it. After you.

(Jude and Matthew exit followed by Gloria. As they do so, Maverick enters)

MAVERICK:
 Everything seems to have gone well.

FELICITY:
 Surprisingly well.

GEMINI:
 I can't believe it myself.

FELICITY: *(playful)*
 Well, I'd better get ready. I'll see you at the altar, hubby.

(Felicity exits)

GEMINI:
 I feel nauseous. I'm doing the right thing. *(To Maverick)* I
 am, right?

MAVERICK:
 Pay no heed to a dying bachelor's words. They mourn for
 deeds they never would have ventured. A fate conceived
 in youth which age doth then undo. As boys, they were
 not taught surrender which maids insist, as men, they do.

GEMINI:
 You're doing it again.

MAVERICK:
 I'm sorry.

GEMINI:
 It's very annoying.

(They exit)

SCENE 19
Matthew's house

(The statue stands alone onstage. Everyone else enters, dancing.)

MATTHEW:
Oh, I've had enough.

GLORIA:
Come on, you're not as old as you look.

MATTHEW:
I am. I am. When I was a boy, the mountains were but molehills.

FELICITY:
You can't quit now.

MATTHEW:
My child, if it were up to me I should dance forever. It's nearing midnight. I'm tired. Go on. Go on! Dance without me.

GEMINI:
Where's Jude? I want to hear a song.

MAVERICK:
Where's my fool?

JUDE:
Here, sir.

MAVERICK:
A request was made of you and I'm inclined to oblige the groom. We would like a song.

123

JUDE:

I'll have to get my guitar.

MAVERICK:

Be quick about it. Fly away little bird.

JUDE:

I need to speak to this lady first.

GLORIA:

Me?

JUDE:

Her name has been muddied lately. And I'm the reason for the slander.

MAVERICK:

If you want to clear her name, do it quickly and be off. You have a job to do if you remember.

JUDE:

I want everyone to know that this lady did me the favor of pretending to love me recently. It was an act of charity on her behalf. I'd decided to kill myself because I thought I couldn't live without her. She, in turn, fawned over me in order to save my life. She knew that if I took time to think about it, I'd come to my senses. She was right. I'd like to thank her for that.

GLORIA:

I did?

JUDE:

She would rather her reputation be ruined than the truth be known.

GLORIA:
> No, I didn't. I don't remember that.

JUDE:
> You did. Don't you remember? You said, 'Jude, I will force myself to love if you will force yourself to live.' And then you were true to your word. I almost believed you myself.

GLORIA:
> I don't remember much about what happened.

JUDE:
> Heroes never do. All the gossip mongers can answer to me from here on out.

GLORIA:
> Well, anyone would have done the same thing in my position.

JUDE:
> You are far too modest.

GLORIA:
> Go get your guitar. We would love to hear you play.

MAVERICK:
> You heard the lady. Get moving!

JUDE:
> Whatever you say.

MAVERICK:
> Hurry up.

JUDE:
> I'm going. I'm going.

(Jude exits)

FELICITY:
> You hate his music.

GLORIA:
> When did I ever say that?

MATTHEW:
> What's all the rush?

FELICITY:
> Nothing, father. We want Jude to play is all. We're all in good spirits and we don't want the night to end.

MATTHEW: *(Melancholy)*
> Yes, how fleeting seems the hour of our good fortune.

MAVERICK:
> And so the mood has ended.

MATTHEW:
> I'm sorry, Felicity. The last thing I want to do is spoil your wedding day.

FELICITY:
> It's almost midnight. The day's almost over.

MATTHEW:
> It is, isn't it? You know, no father could ask his child to be more pleasing to him. I feel honored to have been here in heaven for a time among the angels.

FELICITY:
>
> You sound sad. Don't be sad.

MATTHEW:
>
> Felicity, I've wasted so much time. If only I could do it all again. I would spend each moment without an instant spoiled.

(Bells are heard to ring in the distance)

FELICITY:
>
> What is that? Are those Saint Mary's bells?

GEMINI:
>
> They're coming from that direction.

MATTHEW:
>
> They are. They are! I heard them ring once when I was a boy. Though not so sweetly as they do now. What time is it?

GEMINI:
>
> A minute after twelve.

FELICITY:
>
> Why?

MATTHEW:
>
> I feel reborn, my child. I could dance until the sunrise.

FELICITY:
>
> What's gotten into you?

MATTHEW:
>
> Hope, Felicity. Hope. It appears as if there is hope after all.

GLORIA: *(in the direction of Jude)*
   And friendship.

FELICITY: *(to Gemini)*
   And love.

GEMINI: *(to Felicity)*
   And beauty.

MAVERICK: *(to the group)*
   And truth I fear is lost on you people.

FELICITY:
   Maverick, why do you always have to be so cynical?

GEMINI:
   Don't spoil things, Maverick.

MAVERICK:
   I'm sorry. I'm sorry. You're right. Carry on. As you were.

MATTHEW:
   Where's our musician? I feel like dancing.

FELICITY:
   Who needs him to dance?

MATTHEW:
   As usual, the prettiest girl is also the most astute. If the music won't dance to us, we'll dance to the music.

GEMINI:
   May I?

FELICITY:
   Of course.

(All exit dancing except for Maverick who remains onstage with the statue)

MAVERICK:

It would seem as if we've reached a happy ending. Though ends as these are hardly ends at all. I suppose no one wants to hear that Matthew soon reverted to his old ways. That Gemini and Felicity split up. That Jude died of pancreatic cancer. And Gloria lost the use of her legs in childbirth. I'm not saying it's true. It remains within the realm of possibilities though. But I must confess, despite my melancholy tone and morbid sense of closure, I am still am optimist at heart. Why else would I enjoy a happy ending?

(Maverick kisses the statue, she comes to life, and they both dance off in each others arms)

(Lights out)

Heaven

A play in one act

CHARACTERS

CATHERINE
Big "sister" to Cecelia and Anne; elegant and reserved; loyal.

CECELIA
Rigidly devoted and uncompromising; holds a secret crush on the archangel Gabriel.

ANNE
Naïve younger angel; full of life; curious and sometimes mischievous.

3 ATTENDING ANGELS
Angels who serve The Lord; not particularly graceful or bright.

MEPHISTOPHELES
The devil; well mannered and cultured; debonair; an intellectual with an artistic flair.

THE LORD
God; fatherly; a tad neurotic and impatient at times; a likeable, quirky charm.

THE PUPPY
A puppy.

Heaven
In Heaven

(Enter the angels; CATHERINE, CECELIA, and ANNE)

CATHERINE:
>   Oh, sisters, how my heart trembles.

CECELIA:
>   No peace arrives in company with that dire fool,
>   Mephistopheles.

ANNE:
>   I don't mind him much.

CATHERINE:
>   Whatever so brings his business hither to heaven, angels,
>   we shall refuse purchase.

ANNE:
>   Oh, but Catherine; what if it be roses?

CATHERINE:
>   Yes, especially roses, Anne.

CECELIA:
>   You would sell your soul for a single rose.

ANNE:
>   I would not! Though if he were kind enough to gather
>   one, why should I resent it?

CECELIA:
>   She has a crush on him.

ANNE:
> That is so untrue.

CECELIA:
> Oh, you would sigh longingly for manure had it but a finer smell.

ANNE:
> There is nothing so awful about manure.

CECELIA:
> Why does the Lord even allow this fool admittance unto heaven?

ANNE:
> I'm not a fool.

CECELIA: *(To Anne)*
> Mephistopheles!

CATHERINE:
> He's a longtime friend.

CECELIA:
> A friend? Hah! I'd sooner trust the east winds to blow northerly.

ANNE:
> If he brings a rose I shall accept it. But with such indifference he'll have thought he brought me a toad instead.

CECELIA:
> Could you even distinguish between the two?

ANNE:
> I do so love their little bulgy eyes.

CATHERINE:
> Come, sisters, no time for quibbling now. We must receive our guest graciously.

CECELIA:
> He is not my guest.

CATHERINE:
> Nevertheless.

ANNE: *(Practicing indignation)*
> Humph. A rose? You brought me a rose? Thank you. Thank you. A rose. How nice. Oh, look, a rose.

CECELIA:
> Anne, will you please stop.

CATHERINE:
> Pluck up your wings, angels. I'll not have him ruffle our demeanor. Though he may be allowed to visit the heavens, his footprints shall not soil the clouds beneath. Cecelia, straighten your gown. Anne, don't slouch.

ANNE:
> I'm not slouching.

CATHERINE:
> Here he comes. Posture now.

ANNE:
> I wasn't slouching.

(Enter MEPHISTOPHELES carrying gifts in a bag)

137

MEPHISTOPHELES:

Oh, most beautiful ladies! How longingly have mine eyes been deprived such blessed visions.

CATHERINE:

Mephistopheles.

MEPHISTOPHELES:

My dear Catherine. I must say that I've missed you terribly. And my precious Anne. Tell me, ladies, what offerings may one bestow to angels? I've brought gifts, you see, but I fear you'll find them lacking in some respect. You do reside in heaven, after all. So please, confess to me your most secret wishes and I will make them thine.

CECELIA:

I would wish that you should disappear.

MEPHISTOPHELES:

Cecelia, I'm afraid I have no gift for you.

CECELIA:

You would know little of my desires.

MEPHISTOPHELES:

Strange, I wasn't aware that you possessed them. But as I've said, I have no account for taste only this most accursed appetite. For Catherine, I have a book. And not just any book, mind you. Here are the works of all your favorite poets, novelists, philosophers, and artists in one volume. Of course, I had to omit a few that I simply couldn't stomach, but I still think it's a fair representation.

CATHERINE:
>Thank you, no. I've read them already.

ANNE:
>Well, I shan't be so rude as to refuse your generosity.
>Perchance are those roses for me?

CECELIA:
>Anne!

ANNE:
>How might one be cultured by charity if he is never
>shown?

MEPHISTOPHELES:
>Anne, I would harvest you a billion roses if I thought that
>these few were not enough.

ANNE:
>They're very pretty.

MEPHISTOPHELES:
>Sweet simplicity sprung from such an angel.

CECELIA:
>Oh, how disgusting!

MEPHISTOPHELES:
>You don't agree?

ANNE:
>She's simply jealous.

CECELIA:

> Hardly. My sister seems unable to separate the silkworm
> from the thread it weaves. A thread, I might add, which
> he has spun to be quite transparent.

MEPHISTOPHELES:

> I'm sorry, have I offended you somehow?

ANNE:

> Mephistopheles, the flowers are lovely. Thank you.

MEPHISTOPHELES:

> It was my hope to please you.

ANNE:

> Oh, you did. They're lovely. Really.

CATHERINE:

> What is it you want?

MEPHISTOPHELES:

> Please, Catherine, there's no need to be so direct. We're in
> no hurry, are we? Can't we simply linger awhile in the
> pleasantries of conversation? So, how are you? I haven't
> seen you in awhile.

CATHERINE:

> How am I? Is that all you wish to know? Look before you,
> sisters; there is a saint. To travel such a great distance out
> of consideration for my welfare.

MEPHISTOPHELES:

> Why do you mock me?

CATHERINE:

> I'm afraid I have no choice. Your presence demands it.

MEPHISTOPHELES:
How cruel a weapon is Cupid's bow.

CATHERINE:
You don't love me.

MEPHISTOPHELES:
And how would you know?

CECELIA:
The angels of hell love no one but themselves.

MEPHISTOPHELES:
It's heaven that has no suffering. And therefore, I say, no love. No desire. No passion.

CECELIA:
Go find a harlot in hell, you reptile.

CATHERINE:
Cecelia!

CECELIA:
You are too gracious to him.

MEPHISTOPHELES:
I wouldn't expect you to understand. She who, in life, demanded chastity of her husband.

CECELIA:
An oath he took with pride.

MEPHISTOPHELES:
Given the fate of such a bride.

CECELIA:
> My husband was a saint.

MEPHISTOPHELES:
> That is readily apparent.

CATHERINE:
> Stop it. The both of you.

MEPHISTOPHELES:
> Forgive me, Catherine. My heart has no way with words.
> Somewhere twixt the breast and tongue does truth
> become amended into language.

CATHERINE:
> Oh, please. Spare us the flowery prose. It doesn't become
> you at all. You wear it like a slipper on your elbow. The
> only reason you're here is to satisfy some carnal desire
> you have for me.

MEPHISTOPHELES:
> Catherine, please. There are children present.

CATHERINE:
> Why do you persist? It is wasted effort. Have I not for
> centuries refused you?

MEPHISTOPHELES:
> There's a sadness to your eye.

CATHERINE:
> I assure you I'm quite content.

MEPHISTOPHELES:
> Ah, then it is no wonder. For there is no more wretched
> state than this: contentedness. In truth, you long for me.

CATHERINE:
Perhaps my eyes are only saddened by your presence.

MEPHISTOPHELES:
For it doth cause your fettered heart to stir.

CATHERINE:
Doubtful.

MEPHISTOPHELES:
I have faith.

CATHERINE:
When humility might serve you better.

MEPHISTOPHELES:
Poor Catherine, a stranger to her own desire. Why do you deny that the only evil which reigns, unopposed, is born of your own insane imagination? Oh, Catherine, this is not the place for you. Unencumbered by such things as misery or delight, it suits the souls who have no sense of life. 'Tis hell for she with beauty such as yours. You don't belong here among these lotus-eaters. Immortal parasites. Confess to me your love and be done with it.

CECELIA:
Let's be going, Catherine.

MEPHISTOPHELES:
You weren't prepared were you? For heaven, I mean. You'd forgotten all the pleasures of life. Distracted by its sufferings. And now here, where there is only beauty, you almost envy those who stand outside the gate.

CECELIA:
That's ridiculous!

143

ANNE:
> Mephistopheles, did you bring us another story?

MEPHISTPHELES: *(He pulls a large book from his bag)*
> I would be remiss without one, wouldn't I?

CECELIA:
> I dare say it's not a bible story.

MEPHISTOPHELES:
> No, *this* one has humor in it.

CATHERINE:
> I doubt that we will find it amusing.

ANNE:
> If they don't want to hear, tell me.

MEPHISTOPHELES:
> I can assure you it ends quite happily.

CATHERINE:
> Yes, and your conception of happiness is of the sort I dread.

ANNE:
> Please, Catherine?

MEPHISTOPHELES:
> What else have you to do? Besides, I'm a guest in your home. Are you not obliged to humor me?

CECELIA:
> You were not invited.

MEPHISTOPHELES:
> Quite wrong, as usual. The Lord has summoned me here. I expect He'll be along soon. In the meantime, I see no reason not to grant the child's request.

CATHERINE:
> Oh, very well. But keep it clean.

CECELIA:
> Catherine...

CATHERINE:
> You may leave if you wish, Cecelia.

ANNE:
> What's the story called?

MEPHISTOPHELES:
> I'm not sure. 'The Tiger and the Sheep,' I guess. That's as good a title as any. Not very creative though. Maybe 'Rising above the Herd.' Or "Mediocrity takes a Holiday.'

CATHERINE:
> Get on with it.

(Mephistopheles begins reading as if he were reading to children, holding the book open to show the pictures which accompany the story. The pictures themselves don't necessarily need to be seen by the audience)

MEPHISTOPHELES:
> Very well. Once upon a time, a mother tiger bore a cub and died, leaving the youngster to fend for himself. A herd of sheep found him among the tall grass and took him in, and nursed him.

145

ANNE:
>What was his name?

MEPHISTOPHELES:
>Whose?

ANNE:
>The tiger cub's.

CECELIA:
>Does that matter really?

MEPHISTOPHELES:
>Why, of course it does. Let's see. We'll call him Ismael.

CATHERINE: *(To Mephistopheles)*
>Be careful.

CECELIA:
>I suppose that afterward we should name the whole herd.

MEPHISTOPHELES:
>The sheep are unimportant.

ANNE:
>I like sheep.

CECELIA:
>You see? This story's going to take forever.

MEPHISTOPHELES: *(Reads)*
>The sheep taught young Ismael everything they knew and
>raised him as one of their own. He learned to bleat, to eat
>grass, how to travel among the herd without getting
>stepped on, and visa versa. But as he grew into a rather

impressive figure of a sheep, he was, indeed, quite a sickly creature.

ANNE:
Why is he so sick?

MEPHISTOPHELES:
Improper diet. A tiger's digestive system has no need of grass.

CECELIA:
Will you let him finish?

ANNE:
I need to know these things if I'm going to understand the story.

CATHERINE: *(Gently admonishing)*
Cecelia.

CECELIA: *(Protesting)*
Catherine!

CATHERINE: *(Gesturing for him to continue)*
Mephistopheles.

MEPHISTOPHELES: *(Asking for permission to continue)*
Anne?

ANNE: *(Superior and teasing)*
Cecelia?

CECELIA: *(Protesting)*
Catherine!

CATHERINE:
> Anne! All of you. Stop it.

MEPHISTOPHELES:
> Shall I continue?

ANNE:
> I have one more question.

CECELIA:
> Oh, for the love of...

CATHERINE:
> Hold thy tongue, Cecelia.

MEPHISTOPHELES:
> Of course.

ANNE:
> Why didn't the other sheep know that Ismael was a tiger?

MEPHISTOPHELES:
> They're not the brightest creatures.

CATHERINE:
> It's because they loved him, Anne.

MEPHISTOPHELES:
> That is true, they loved him entirely. *(To Catherine)* And sometimes love, they say, can make one blind.

CATHERINE: *(To Mephistopheles)*
> Or delusional.

MEPHISTOPHELES: *(Reads)*
> Well, Ismael was with the sheep for about a year, when
> one day another male tiger, and this one a great deal
> older than he, came pouncing on the herd. Of course, they
> scattered and fled into the hills. But Ismael, he was a tiger
> after all, stood still and stared at the creature in
> amazement. 'Good gracious!' growled the older tiger
> 'What are you doing here living with these sheep?' But
> Ismael could only answer: 'Baaaaaaaa.' Of course, this
> mortified the elder cat and Ismael, embarrassed, began to
> nibble on the grass. The big fellow becomes enraged by
> now and begins to beat Ismael about the ears a few times.

ANNE:
> Now, that's just mean.

MEPHISTOPHELES: *(Continues reading)*
> He picks the smaller tiger up and takes him by the neck to
> a crystal clear pond. 'Now look' he demands, and the little
> one peeks his head out over the glassy pool. For the first
> time Ismael sees his face. The older tiger then stands
> beside him and both animals are reflected in the still
> waters. 'You see? You're like me.' says the elder 'You've
> the face of a tiger. We both are tigers.' He then escorts
> little Ismael to his den where there lay a recently
> slaughtered gazelle. He tears a chunk of meat from off the
> body and offers it to Ismael. 'Now open your face!' the
> elder demands. 'But I'm a vegetarian.' the little one cries.
> 'Enough with this nonsense! Now here!' And he shoves
> the meat down the younger tiger's throat. Of course, the
> little one gags at first. But soon Ismael begins to grow
> stronger, fortified by his proper diet. And after awhile he
> lets out a roar. A small one. Though in no time his voice
> was to be heard echoing loudly throughout the jungle.

(Pause)

149

The end.

CECELIA:
That's it?

ANNE:
What happened to him then?

MEPHISTOPHELES:
I suppose he lived happily after. If you believe in that sort of thing.

ANNE:
What about the sheep?

MEPHISTOPHELES:
They continued grazing, I guess. Sheep do that.

CECELIA:
I've never heard a more ridiculous story.

MEPHISTOPHELES:
Have you not read the bible?

CECELIA:
For one thing, animals do not speak.

MEPHISTOPHELES:
And burning bushes do?

CECELIA:
The word of God can hardly be compared.

MEPHISTOPHELES:
It's a parable.

CECELIA:
>Though one is true and the other isn't.

MEPHISTOPHELES:
>So, you believe Moses parted the sea?

CECELIA:
>Precisely.

MEPHISTOPHELES:
>And in such a world of burning bushes and oceanic miracles, you find it impossible to conceive of a speaking tiger?

CECELIA:
>And whoever heard of jungle sheep?

ANNE:
>I liked the story.

CECELIA:
>You would.

(Enter THE LORD encircled by a group of ATTENDING ANGELS who dance around Him, smiling wildly, spritzing Him with perfume and adorning Him with flower petals. CATHERINE, CECELIA, and ANNE are frozen by the sight of Him)

THE LORD: *(Clapping)*
>Bravo, my friend. Bravo! You always were one to spin a tale. Usually lies, but nevertheless.

MEPHISTOPHELES: *(Bowing)*
>My Lord.

(THE LORD snaps His fingers and the three angels are woken from their trance)

THE LORD:
>Do you know the story about the tiger and the bounty hunter?

MEPHISTOPHELES:
>You don't need to be sarcastic.

THE LORD:
>You speak with such eloquence when it suits you. Why is it that you don't reserve such a poetic disposition for the rest of us?

MEPHISTOPHELES:
>You wanted to see me?

THE LORD:
>I did? That's right, I did. I need your help with a rather important matter.

MEPHISTOPHELES:
>My help?

THE LORD: *(Taking Mephistopheles aside)*
>Strange, I know, given my omnipotence. However, this is a problem that perhaps only you might solve for me. It seems that I have lost my creative spirit. I'm blocked. I couldn't make a platypus if my reputation depended upon it. As you can see, I need your assistance here.

MEPHISTOPHELES:
>What do you think is the problem?

THE LORD:
> I've just told you the problem. I need the solution. I need something to challenge me to excellence again. I'm slipping, man.

MEPHISTOPHELES:
> What are you talking about?

THE LORD:
> Cecelia, think of a number between infinity and one. The first that comes to you.

CECELIA:
> I have it, my Lord.

THE LORD: *(Disappointed)*
> Is it: two?

CECELIA:
> It is!

ATTENDING ANGELS: *(suddenly breaking into song)*
> Hallelujah!

THE LORD:
> That's enough.

ATTENDING ANGELS:
> Hallelujah! Hallelujah!

MEPHISTOPHELES:
> I see what you mean.

ATTENDING ANGELS:
> Hallelujah!

THE LORD: *(He snaps His fingers and the angels all freeze)*
  I said, enough!

  (He snaps his fingers again and they all unfreeze)

MEPHISTOPHELES:
  They only mean to praise you.

THE LORD:
  I'm so utterly bored with it. Where have you been, my
  friend? I've missed you terribly.

CECELIA:
  Him?

THE LORD:
  These angels are far too easily impressed.

MEPHISTOPHELES:
  They do *mean* well.

THE LORD:
  Mistake me not. I love them. They're my children. I miss
  the old days though. There's no challenge anymore since
  you left. A game of chess is utterly depressing. I would
  feign to lose except the damage it might do to my
  reputation. You should return to us.

MEPHISTOPHELES:
  I'm afraid that would be impossible.

THE LORD:
  How long have you been gone?

MEPHISTOPHELES:
  It's been awhile, my Lord.

THE LORD:
It seems like only yesterday.

MEPHISTOPHELES:
To you it would.

THE LORD:
Don't be so contemptuous.

MEPHISTOPHELES:
I'm afraid that cynicism is in my nature.

THE LORD:
It's rather aggravating.

MEPHISTOPHELES:
So you see we still remain at an impasse.

THE LORD:
You might choose to loosen your horns a bit.

MEPHISTOPHELES:
It's you who gave them to me. Besides, I've sacrificed enough.

THE LORD:
Do you believe my burden is an easy one to bear? I know all. I see all.

MEPHISTOPHELES:
Yes, you're Santa Claus.

THE LORD:
Make sport at my expense. I'll allow it. If for no other reason than it might relieve me from this tediousness.

MEPHISTOPHELES:
You conceived of heaven, not I. If it does not please you, alter it.

THE LORD:
You're so naïve. Why else do you believe I created the world?

MEPHISTOPHELES:
To amuse yourself?

THE LORD:
Precisely. So much happens there to surprise me. It's all a wonderful play. It's supposed to be, anyway. I don't know what's happened to it lately. Everyone now spends half their days sitting in front of some sort of screen. No one has any need for me anymore unless they're dying or their mortgage is past due.

MEPHISTOPHELES:
I thought it was all part of some master plan.

THE LORD:
Don't be ridiculous. I created life, they did everything else. Any fool can write a book. Only I have created something that then creates itself. That regenerates and reorganizes and moves forward in a billion different directions all at once. Why, in my own name, would I make something so pedestrian as to be preordained? It's all a variation on a theme. I know the theme. It's the variations which I find interesting. The problem, of course, is what to do for an encore.

MEPHISTOPHELES:
So there is a theme then?

THE LORD:
> Of course there's a theme. There'd be no order to it without a theme.

MEPHISTOPHELES:
> Can you tell it to me?

THE LORD:
> You're always looking for an angle aren't you, my friend? I'm afraid you wouldn't understand it anyway.

MEPHISTOPHELES:
> You never know. I might surprise you.

THE LORD:
> Very well.

(THE LORD opens his mouth and begins to "speak" the beginning of Bach's Brandenburg concerto # 3 while the ATTENDING ANGELS flit about the stage. Again CATHERINE, CECELIA, and ANNE are frozen with amazement. Once finished, THE LORD snaps his fingers to awaken them)

> Shall I continue?

ANNE:
> Oh, yes!

MEPHISTOPHELES:
> You're being deliberately vague.

ANNE:
> It's beautiful.

MEPHISTOPHELES:
It's Bach.

THE LORD:
You see? It's quite incomprehensible. And we've yet to
even touch upon chaos theory. Have you any idea how
lonely I am?

MEPHISTOPHELES:
It's tough to be the king.

THE LORD:
How true. Though it does have certain advantages.

MEPHISTOPHELES:
I'm sure.

THE LORD:
Mephistopheles, I'm desperate.

CECELIA:
My Lord, if I may humbly speak my mind?

MEPHISTOPHELES:
Why, Cecelia, what a refreshing change. An original
thought?

THE LORD:
Of course you may.

CECELIA:
This angel, by you, was banished from here. Why do you
now allow him to return?

THE LORD:
He was my favorite.

CECELIA:
> And he betrayed you.

MEPHISTOPHELES:
> I don't remember that you were there.

CECELIA:
> Gabriel has told me.

MEPHISTOPHELES:
> The ruffian.

ANNE:
> Oh, Gabriel. Gabriel. Gabriel. Can you speak of no one else?

CATHERINE:
> Anne!

CECELIA:
> I beg your pardon.

ANNE:
> She speaks as if he were a God. No offense.

THE LORD:
> None taken.

ANNE:
> No wing might make compare to Gabriel's. No arm as strong. No eye as blue.

CECELIA:
> You're making a fool of yourself.

ANNE:
>   Am I? Or is it you?

CECELIA:
>   What are you talking about?

ANNE:
>   Your love for Gabriel.

CECELIA:
>   Untrue!

ANNE:
>   'Tis so.

CECELIA:
>   Untrue! You malicious little brat.

ANNE:
>   Ah, you're blushing.

CECELIA:
>   I am most certainly *not* blushing.

ANNE:
>   Oh please! All of heaven knows of it but you and Gabriel himself.

CECELIA:
>   You're all a rotten bunch of gossips then.

ANNE:
>   I think you should tell him.

CECELIA:
>   What should I say of nothing?

ANNE:
> Throw yourself upon his feet and say: 'Oh, Gabriel, I adore you!'

CATHERINE:
> Enough! The both of you! See what you've started?

MEPHISTOPHELES:
> How am I to blame?

CATHERINE:
> Your presence alone stirs up these forces.

THE LORD:
> It's true. You do.

CECELIA:
> See? I told you not to accept that rose.

ANNE:
> If you should notice, I'm ignoring you.

CATHERINE:
> Angels, please! *(To Mephistopheles)* You should be ashamed.

MEPHISTOPHELES:
> Me?

THE LORD:
> Children. Children, please. Enough bickering.

ATTENDING ANGELS:
> The Lord has spoken. So sayeth the Lord. Hallelujah!

THE LORD:
> That's unnecessary.

ATTENDING ANGELS:
> Hallelujah! Hallelujah!

THE LORD: *(Loudly)*
> Enough!

ATTENDING ANGELS: *(Very meekly)*
> Hallelujah.

THE LORD:
> I suppose you should state your business here, my friend.
> It seems my angels are feeling the stress of your arrival.

MEPHISTOPHELES:
> You called me here.

THE LORD:
> That's right, so I did.

MEPHISTOPHELES:
> Though I do have another matter I must discuss with you.

THE LORD:
> I knew you would. It's about the souls I took from you in
> Hell, isn't it?

MEPHISTOPHELES:
> And those with whom you've chosen to replace them.

THE LORD:
> It was a fair trade.

MEPHISTOPHELES:
Hardly. They're miserable, my Lord. They don't belong.
As I'm sure are those souls now here in heaven miserable.

CECELIA:
How dare you say that any soul in Heaven is miserable.

MEPHISTOPHELES:
Cecelia, for some, my Hell, to them, is as blissful as this,
your Heaven, is to you.

CECELIA:
My Lord?

THE LORD:
He's speaking metaphorically.

(Pulling MEPHISTOPHELES aside)

There are some things these angels need not know. Why
destroy their confidence? For spite?

MEPHISTOPHELES:
My Lord, I might as well bellow into the winds as speak a
truth upon the ears of one who would not hear me.

THE LORD: *(To the angels)*
Angels, you must consider the devil your source, before
you should rush to judgment of our conversations here. I
expect you are unable to fully comprehend the
circumstances of which we speak.

CECELIA:
Oh, my Lord, forgive me for listening to this devil here.

163

Heaven

THE LORD: *(To the attending angels)*
Absolve her.

(The ATTENDING ANGELS break into Motown-style revival hymnals and dance around the kneeling Cecelia while they spritz her with perfume and cover her with flower petals, occasionally bumping into one another in the process)

Now, as you were saying?

MEPHISTOPHELES:
You've taken Goethe, Shakespeare, and Homer from me and replaced them with three of the most annoying Bishops I've ever met.

THE LORD:
They're very accomplished men.

MEPHISTOPHELES:
That's beside the point. They don't belong.

THE LORD:
I need them at the moment. I've told you, I need some inspiration. I'm having problems.

MEPHISTOPHELES:
All of them? You've taken nearly a thousand souls.

THE LORD:
Yes, all of them. Though I'll admit it hasn't been going well. Don't worry, I intend to return them eventually.

MEPHISTOPHELES:
Of course it isn't going well. They aren't able to thrive in Heaven. They're miserable. Like the Jesuits you sent me. They're having a terrible time with the prostitutes of Hell.

THE LORD:
>Why should this disturb you so? It's only temporary.
>Besides they're all men and women who excelled in some
>fashion.

MEPHISTOPHELES:
>It's a matter of degree, my Lord. You know that. Success
>among the living has nothing to do with it. Ms. Dickinson
>resided there long before her name was known to poetry.
>And Danielle Steel would be out of place should she
>prosper for another hundred years.

ANNE:
>Is Van Gogh among the souls in Hell?

MEPHISTOPHELES:
>He was, yes.

ANNE:
>You were right.

CECELIA:
>I told you.

ANNE:
>How about Elvis?

MEPHISTOPHELES:
>He is now, unfortunately. Thanks to your sovereign here.
>I do believe that Hell has come to be defined as sharing a
>toilet with Elvis. He wanders sometimes to Kalamazoo
>and we do little to stop him.

ANNE:
>Is Hell then full of artists?

CECELIA:
They're the greatest sinners, Anne.

CATHERINE:
Cecelia, no one is speaking to you.

CECELIA:
I'm only trying to help.

CATHERINE:
Well, stop it.

MEPHISTOPHELES:
Hell is full of lovers, Anne. Not artists.

CECELIA:
A bunch of fornicators if you ask me.

CATHERINE:
Cecelia!

CECELIA:
Are you listening to him? He's mocking us. He's mocking *you*, my Lord.

(The ATTENDING ANGELS each take on a pose of "speak, see, and hear no evil")

THE LORD:
I appreciate your concern, Cecelia.

CECELIA:
Am I the only one who's outraged here? My Lord, let us remove him back to Hell from whence he came. If he should find it so enjoyable, let him stay there.

MEPHISTOPHELES:
> I mean no disrespect. Well, perhaps I do, but not
> intentionally.

THE LORD:
> I'm afraid those souls I've sent to Hell must remain there.
> At least for the time being.

MEPHISTOPHELES:
> I entreat you, Lord...

THE LORD:
> Mephistopheles, I would suggest you keep an open mind.
> These are souls with attributes fine enough. Perhaps not
> so refined as some that you might deem admirable, but
> they will serve. Why must you be so discriminating?

MEPHISTOPHELES:
> I have my pride.

THE LORD:
> You were banished from here because of it.

MEPHISTOPHELES:
> And if memory serves, because I would not bow to man.

THE LORD:
> And *why* wouldn't you?

MEPHISTOPHELES:
> I will admit there are a few that I admire. However, the
> vast majority are lazier than a caterpillar. And yet it
> doesn't seem to trouble them in the least. They even
> laugh at it. No wonder they believe themselves to be
> divinely blessed. By all assurances they should have
> starved to death long ago.

THE LORD:
>   If you find them so disdainful, why should you care if they
>   are miserable?

MEPHISTOPHELES:
>   Hell is my refuge, Lord. My sanctuary. In heaven was I
>   made to suffer every slack-jawed fool. Every coward who
>   then you would place upon a pedestal. In Hell, I'm
>   surrounded by those who are the most like me.

THE LORD:
>   'No beast so fierce but that knows some touch of pity.'

MEPHISTOPHELES:
>   Stolen from he who was stolen from me by you.

THE LORD:
>   I do enjoy quoting Shakespeare. I love that line.
>   Sometimes I'll speak it for no reason whatsoever.

MEPHISTOPHELES:
>   Obviously.

THE LORD:
>   I like the way it rolls off my tongue. 'No beast so fierce but
>   that knows some touch of pity'.

(The following exchange slowly begins to evolve into a competition of sorts)

MEPHISTOPHELES:
>   'But I know none and therefore am no beast.'

THE LORD:
> 'Some evil beast shall then devour him'

(The ATTENDING ANGELS sound 'Amen')

MEPHISTOPHELES:
> 'And what rough beast, its hour come round at last,
> slouches towards Bethlehem to be born?'

(The ATTENDING ANGELS begin to hiss quietly)

THE LORD:
> 'The quality of mercy is not strained,
> it dropeth as the gentle rain from heaven
> upon the place beneath: it is twice blest;
> it blesseth him that gives and him that takes:
> 'Tis mightiest in the mightiest; it becomes
> the throned monarch better than his crown.'

(The ATTENDING ANGELS sound 'hallelujah')

MEPHISTOPHELES:
> 'I am too proud to be a parasite
> and if my nature wants the germ that grows
> towering to heaven like the mountain pine
> or like the oak - sheltering multitudes,
> I stand, not high it may be - but alone!'

(One ATTENDING ANGEL sounds a meager 'Booooo')

(Pause)

ANNE:
> 'Gallop apace you fiery footed steeds,
> towards Phoebus' lodging; such a wagoner
> As Phaeton would whip you to the west

169

and bring in cloudy night immediately.
Spread thy close curtain, love performing night!
That runaway's eyes may wink, and Romeo
Leap to these arms, untalked of and unseen!'

(All pause to stare at ANNE then, altogether, return to their conversation)

THE LORD:
You see, my friend? This is why I need your company.
You inspire me.

MEPHISTOPHELES:
I inspire you to quotation?

THE LORD:
Don't make light of the situation, Mephistopheles. This is serious. I've been agonizing for centuries over what to do. But you're right, I can't conceive of an original thought. I take credit for the ideas of Shakespeare and Homer as if they were my own. I suppose by genealogy they can be traced to me, but how pathetic.

MEPHISTOPHELES:
Do you remember when you first created the universe?

THE LORD:
I've been resting on those laurels ever since.

MEPHISTOPHELES:
You were tortured then as well.

THE LORD:
Was I?

MEPHISTOPHELES:
> It's an important part of the process. Like having to recreate everything all over again from scratch.

THE LORD:
> Interesting.

MEPHISTOPHELES:
> Remember the story of Jacob? Jacob once wrestled with an angel until the break of day. Even after the angel wrenched his hip out of joint, he still wrestled with him. And the angel said, 'let me go for it's nearly dawn.' And Jacob said, 'No, I will not let thee go. Not until you bless me.'

THE LORD:
> Of course! How could I have been so blind? You're right. I need to wrestle an angel.

(The attending angels all freeze in terror. There's a brief moment of indecisiveness before they all exit wildly screaming).

MEPHISTOPHELES:
> I think you're missing the point, my Lord.

(The Lord begins to stalk Mephistopheles in a circle, as if to pounce on him)

THE LORD:
> It's been a long time, Mephistopheles.

MEPHISTOPHELES:
> I'm not going to wrestle with you again.

THE LORD:
> You know you want to.

MEPHISTOPHELES:
> Don't be absurd.

THE LORD:
> You want me to return your souls to Hell?

MEPHISTOPHELES:
> I'm not about to make the same mistake twice.

THE LORD:
> That was a long time ago. I'm not as strong as I used to be.

MEPHISTOPHELES:
> It's not my forte.

THE LORD:
> Oh, come on.

MEPHISTOPHELES:
> It's not a fair fight. I'm an intellectual.

THE LORD:
> Doesn't it bother you that I'm more popular? You're responsible for the advent of every great innovation known to man and I get all the glory for it. That must be maddening.

MEPHISTOPHELES:
> Please, you're insulting my intelligence.

THE LORD:
> Bless me.

MEPHISTOPHELES:
> You're making a spectacle of yourself.

THE LORD:
> Bless me!

MEPHISTOPHELES:
> My Lord, I am no longer an angel.

THE LORD:
> I said, bless me, damn you!

(The Lord lunges at Mephistopheles and they wrestle. A series of quick blackouts and fade ups with the lights, as well as the repositioning of actors during these short periods of darkness into odd poses, should provide a comical effect and give the illusion that a great deal of time passes during their wrestling match.)

(THE LORD finally pins MEPHISTOPHELES)

> Say it! Say it!

MEPHISTOPHELES:
> Alright! Alright! I bless you, for crying out loud! I bless you! I bless you!

THE LORD:
> I knew you would.

MEPHISTOPHELES:
> It still doesn't solve your problem.

THE LORD:
> On the contrary, I feel much better.

MEPHISTOPHELES:
> I'm so glad that I could help.

THE LORD:
> I think I've been looking at this thing all wrong. I've been thinking that I need to create something tangible. Like the universe. Something physical and concrete. But what could be more challenging than to recreate myself? What greater accomplishment? Angels, I need you.

(The attending angels rush back to the Lord's side)

ATTENDING ANGELS:
> Yes, my Lord?

THE LORD:
> I've been out of touch with my constituency. What are people on earth worshipping these days?

ANGEL #1:
> Television.

THE LORD:
> As a deity, I mean.

ANGEL #2
> Television.

THE LORD:
> No, what do they believe in? What makes it possible for them to get out of bed in the morning?

ANGEL #3:
> Therapy?

THE LORD:
> Go. Bring me back a creature from earth.

(The three angels disappear in a flash)

MEPHISTOPHELES:
> What are you doing?

THE LORD:
> Going directly to the source.

(The three angels return)

ANGELS:
> My Lord!

THE LORD:
> What took you so long?

ANGELS:
> As you requested.

(They hand the Lord a small puppy. Immediately all of the angels gather around the dog with excitement, cooing with affection)

THE LORD:
> What is this?

ANGEL #1:
> A creature from earth, my Lord.

THE LORD:
> True. It is. But I think you misunderstood me.

175

ANGEL #2:
> Isn't he adorable?

THE LORD:
> Again. Not the point.

ANGEL #3:
> I told you we should have taken the wolverine.

ANGEL #2:
> His name is Stan.

THE LORD:
> A wolverine named Stan?

ANGEL #2:
> No, the puppy's name is Stan.

ANGEL #1:
> The wolverine's name was Beatrice.

ANNE:
> Oh, that's so pretty. I once had a duck named Beatrice.

THE LORD:
> Enough already!

CATHERINE:
> My Lord, you're scaring him.

ANGEL #1:
> Puppies have very sensitive ears.

CECELIA:
> It's okay, Stan. It's okay.

ANNE: *(To the Lord)*
    Shame on you. You should know better.

THE LORD:
    I've been upstaged by a mutt.

ANGEL #1:
    He's not a mutt.

ANGEL#2:
    I'm sure he's a pure-bred something or other.

ANGEL #3:
    And even if he is a mutt, we still love him, don't we, Stan?

THE LORD:
    Ladies, let's focus here please.

ANGEL #1:
    Can we keep him, My Lord? Can we?

THE LORD:
    Absolutely not.

ANGEL #2:
    Please? We'll take good care of him.

ANGEL #3:
    We'll do everything.

THE LORD:
    That's what you said about the Llama and the Polynesian mountain goat. And who's taking care of them right now?

ANGEL #2:
    Noah.

THE LORD:
> That's right. Noah. You think he has time for a puppy as well? We've burdened that poor man enough.

ANGEL #1:
> I guess not.

THE LORD:
> Besides, isn't there someone on earth who might need him more than you? A child, perhaps? Someone who could use a friend as good as this one?

ANGEL #2:
> I suppose.

THE LORD:
> Why don't you go take him back?

> *(Angel #1 disappears to return the puppy)*

> Perhaps I should approach this a different way.

> *(Angel #1 returns again without the puppy)*

MEPHISTOPHELES:
> You could return things to the way they were.

THE LORD:
> Cecelia, when you look at me what do you see?

CECELIA:
> I don't understand, my Lord.

THE LORD:
>   I am many things to many different people. But what specifically do you see when you look at me? How do I look to you?

CECELIA:
>   Like the most beautiful woman I've ever seen.

THE LORD:
>   A woman? Interesting.

MEPHISTOPHELES:
>   What are you trying to do?

THE LORD:
>   I'm gathering information, my friend. Perhaps some revelation to inspire me.

MEPHISTOPHELES:
>   Do you see a woman here, Catherine?

CATHERINE:
>   Of course I do.

MEPHISTOPHELES:
>   Anne?

ANNE:
>   I see a spirit of light surrounded by a trillion stars in darkness.

MEPHISTOPHELES:
>   Angels?

ATTENDING ANGEL #1:
>   I see a lion. But She's most definitely a female.

179

ATTENDING ANGEL #2:
> The Lord seems androgynous to me.

THE LORD:
> Interesting.

ATTENDING ANGEL #2:
> No offense.

THE LORD:
> By all means.

ATTENDING ANGEL #2:
> If I must choose, I'd say a woman.

THE LORD:
> Would you?

ATTENDING ANGEL #2:
> Well, you have a lot of hair, my Lord.

THE LORD:
> Do I?

ATTENDING ANGEL #2
> Perhaps. Oh wait, I see it now. A man! I was confused.

THE LORD:
> I am?

ATTENDING ANGEL #2:
> Aren't you?

THE LORD:
> You tell me.

ATTENDING ANGEL #2:
   I don't want to play anymore.

THE LORD:
   What about you?

ATTENDING ANGEL #3:
   I'd rather not say, my Lord.

THE LORD:
   Oh, come on.

ATTENDING ANGEL #3:
   You promise not to hold it against me?

THE LORD:
   Of course.

ATTENDING ANGEL #3:
   They all must promise not to laugh.

THE LORD:
   I assure you.

ATTENDING ANGEL #3:
   Him too?

MEPHISTOPHELES:
   My laughter is spontaneous. It's wholly out of my control.

THE LORD:
   Ignore him. Tell me.

ATTENDING ANGEL #3:
   Well, my Lord, you do appear, and I in no way claim
   authority of vision, as if, and this is subject to debate of

course, you were a satyr. Half man, half beast. Sometimes you're black. Other times you're red. I admit that I avert my eyes on occasion because, quite frankly, you scare me a little.

THE LORD:
Have I a tail?

ATTENDING ANGEL #3:
Oh no, my Lord.

THE LORD:
Too bad.

ATTENDING ANGEL #3:
Perhaps you do. If I were to look closer.

THE LORD:
I do?

ATTENDING ANGEL #3:
Yes, I don't know how I could have missed it. It's a magnificent tail.

MEPHISTOPHELES:
And I'm accused of vacillation.

CECELIA:
Potty mouth.

THE LORD:
Very interesting. Very interesting indeed. I'm not sure where it will lead me, but definitely material for consideration.

MEPHISTOPHELES:
> These are all very superficial factors.

THE LORD:
> Yes, but I must keep up with the times. I haven't been,
> you see. That's why people have lost their use for me.

MEPHISTOPHELES:
> So eradicate them. Start over. There's a creative project
> for you.

THE LORD:
> I can't. I made a promise to Noah that I wouldn't do that
> again.

MEPHISTOPHELES:
> So what? You're God. What is he going to do?

THE LORD:
> It wouldn't look good.

MEPHISTOPHELES:
> You've become a slave to fashion.

THE LORD:
> It beats being alone.

MEPHISTOPHELES:
> My Lord, I hate to break this to you, but you are the Lord
> God and no matter how you may try to lower yourself to
> the level of humanity, it doesn't change that one
> important fact. You've already let these people make you
> into a neurotic shadow of your former self. You are alone.
> You're alone because those who are exalted above the
> multitudes, who possess qualities rarefied and fashioned
> by a singular mold, must necessarily stand alone. They

are a refutation to mediocrity. And mediocrity is the only devil of which I know.

THE LORD:
I'm listening.

MEPHISTOPHELES:
You are not a creative God, you're a disciplinarian. You strike fear into the hearts of men and women and it's this fear that keeps the majority of them from tearing each other completely to pieces.

THE LORD:
I must say, I am starting to feel invigorated again. Let me try something.

(Steps to the front edge of the stage and looks down as if peering into the world of mortals)

Cecilia, come here.

CECELIA:
Yes, my Lord.

THE LORD: *(pointing to the mortals below)*
You seem to know the sinners well, direct me to an adulterer.

CECELIA: *(Pointing emphatically)*
Him, my Lord! The one down there, copulating with his wife's obstetrician.

THE LORD:
Repugnant sinners!!

(The Lord raises his hands and suspends them there in midair in preparation for the powerful thunderbolts that he is about to unleash from his fingertips. He then lets the thunderbolts loose upon the two unfortunates of earth as the stage lights flicker wildly and the loud crashing of thunder can be heard). Author's note: the duration of this episode can be exaggerated for greater comic effect.

CECELIA:
Wow!

ATTENDING ANGELS:
Awesome!

THE LORD: *(Excited)*
You're right, Mephistopheles. This is invigorating. Everything is renewed. Who else can I eviscerate?

MEPHISTOPHELES:
Pace yourself.

ANNE: *(Looking down at the destruction of the sinners)*
They look like two pieces of coal melted together.

THE LORD:
Why, Anne, that's a beautiful rose that you have there. I hadn't noticed it.

ANNE:
Mephistopheles gave it to me.

THE LORD:
Did he?

ANNE:
Charitably, I accepted it.

Heaven

THE LORD:
> It's very pretty.

ANNE:
> It's beginning to die already.

THE LORD:
> Let me see it.

(The Lord runs his fingers over the flower's petals)

> Pale death has no dominion here. Look.

ATTENDING ANGELS:
> Hallelujah!

THE LORD:
> You must excuse me, Mephistopheles. I have a great deal
> of work to do. So many sinners, so little time.

MEPHISTOPHELES:
> What about the souls you've stolen from me?

THE LORD:
> I have no more need of them. I'll see that they're returned
> to you at once. Come, angels. We're going to need a cage,
> a blowtorch, and two unscrupulously bred and trained
> Australian cobra ferrets. The United Nations is going to
> be in session soon.

*(The ATTENDING ANGELS exit with THE LORD singing
lively spirituals and adorning him again with flower petals)*

CATHERINE:
> We should be going as well, sisters.

MEPHISTOPHELES:
Catherine, wait.

CATHERINE:
We're required to stay no longer.

CECELIA:
Don't make me call on Gabriel.

ANNE:
Oh, yes, for Gabriel is so splendid! For Gabriel's above the moon. How gorgeous is my Gabriel.

CECELIA:
Now *I* am ignoring *you*.

ANNE:
Hush! Methinks I heard the sigh of Gabriel. Run, Mephistopheles. Run!

CATHERINE:
Anne, please.

CECELIA:
You're making a fool of yourself.

ANNE:
I'm just reveling in the sound of his name. Gabriel. Gabriel. Gabriel.

CECELIA:
Are you amusing yourself?

ANNE:
I'd have to say I am.

CECELIA:
I have more important things to do.

(Cecelia exits)

ANNE:
Say hello to Gabriel for me

CATHERINE:
Stop saying "Gabriel." He's bound to come rushing over here in full battle gear.

MEPHISTOPHELES:
Must you leave so soon, Catherine?

CATHERINE:
We've stayed too long as it is.

MEPHISTOPHELES:
My offer still stands.

CATHERINE:
To join your souls in Hell? No, thank you.

MEPHISTOPHELES:
Well, perhaps a fling into the underworld. Who said love should last for all eternity?

CATHERINE:
Another tempting offer which I must decline.

MEPHISTOPHELES:
A pity.

CATHERINE:
For some of us.

MEPHISTOPHELES:
> Well, a hundred times for every man in love is there a man alone. And so for angels.

CATHERINE:
> I suppose that's true.

MEPHISTOPHELES:
> Inevitably. Farewell, my Catherine. Enjoy your eternal life of ease. The lotus trees await you. I only hope you may digest them.

CATHERINE:
> You make it seem so undesirable.

MEPHISTOPHELES:
> To she unknown to passion, it may only seem as her reward.

CATHERINE:
> Goodbye, Mephistopheles.

MEPHISTOPHELES:
> May I request a kiss before you leave?

CATHERINE:
> That would be inappropriate.

MEPHISTOPHELES:
> Are you afraid?

CATHERINE:
> Of what?

MEPHISTOPHELES:
> One kiss. My lips.

CATHERINE:
    I hardly think so.

MEPHISTOPHELES:
    Perhaps you find me irresistible. I'll prove it to you.

CATHERINE:
    By kissing me?

MEPHISTOPHELES:
    Once kissed was she twice blest. And he as well. And all
    the world was left to nothing.

CATHERINE:
    I don't think so.

MEPHISTOPHELES:
    Goodbye then, Catherine.

CATHERINE:
    Goodbye. Come along Anne.

*(The two angels exit leaving MEPHISTOPHELES alone
onstage. Suddenly ANNE returns and kisses him passionately,
then saunters off with a smile, smelling her rose)*

MEPHISTOPHELES: *(To audience)*
    Oh, please. Like I don't know who you've been kissing.

(Lights out)

About the Author

Emile Benoit is a writer and teacher living in California. He holds B.A. and M.A. degrees in philosophy from San Diego State University and spent 12 years as an actor working in regional theatres across the country. His next book entitled *The Eudaimon: Essays and Aphorisms on the Higher Man* will be released in December of 2011.

Heaven